Raise
the Bottom

How to Keep Secret Alcoholics
from Damaging Your Business

Raise
the Bottom

How to Keep Secret Alcoholics
from Damaging Your Business

Arthur M. Jackson

Bascom Hill Books
212 3rd Avenue North, Suite 570
Minneapolis, MN 55401
612.455.2293
www.bascomhillpublishing.com

ISBN - 978-0-9820938-2-5
ISBN - 0-9820938-2-9
LCCN - 2008941119

Order Fulfilment Center:
Blu Sky Media Group, Inc.
P.O. Box 10069
Murfreesboro, TN 37129
Toll Free: 1-888-448-BSMG (2764)
Phone: 615-995-7072
Fax: 615-217-3088
E-Mail: info@bluskymediagroup.com

Printed in the United States of America

BASCOM
HILL BOOKS

Dedicated to my wonderful parents
Allen and Miriam Jackson

Table of Contents

Introduction

Alcoholism is rampant, but due to its stigma, people rarely discuss it. *Raise the Bottom* explains the real danger of alcoholism—the significant impact of alcoholic thinking and behavior, whether a person is under the influence or not.

Raise the Bottom is a business book, not a recovery book. It covers Step Zero, the real beginning of any program of recovery.

Through two main characters, Jason Burke, a recent MBA graduate from a well-known East Coast business school, and Aaron Middleton, a veteran, highly accomplished business consultant, you will learn to see and think differently about many common business problems. In *Raise the Bottom* Jason's knowledge of alcoholism evolves and matures beyond the range of his preconceptions and cynicism, typical of the general public, to the point that he is able to connect the dots between the disease, the behavior, and the bottom line—and to propose effective steps to a solution.

In Part One, Aaron and Jason discuss the problems created by alcoholism in the work environment, covering biological factors, definitions of alcoholism, and stages in the progress of the disease. In Part Two, Aaron teaches Jason how to identify alcoholism—often long before the alcoholic himself is aware he has a problem. Part Three closes with concrete responses to the problem, including disenabling the alcoholic, and the other steps necessary to protect yourself and your workplace from the damage an alcoholic employee can cause.

My twenty-plus years experience in business and marketing consulting has provided me with wide exposure to many diverse business situations. As a recovering alcoholic, I can see in retrospect that many of the problems I tackled were actually the result of alcoholic thinking and behavior. However, all the stories and characters are fictional. Any similarity to real places or people is purely coincidental.

The premise of *Raise the Bottom,* like that of most treatment programs, is that an alcoholic must hit bottom before he can change. As one of the co-founders of Alcoholics Anonymous pointed out, we can effectively raise that bottom and intervene in the progress of the disease, reducing the harm done to the alcoholic and to a business. This is the goal of *Raise the Bottom*.

I hope that this book will demystify alcoholism and help business people guide those suffering from the disease get help. Should you see yourself in this book and wonder whether you are an alcoholic, take advantage of the insight and take corrective actions now. It will save you and others great distress later.

Thank you for taking the time to learn more about one of the leading social problems of our time.

Arthur Jackson

A Note on the Style

Throughout this book, I refer to alcoholics in the masculine third person, he or him. I follow this tradition as a more graceful reference than *he or she*, for instance, or *s/he* or, worst of all, *them*.

I advise the reader that alcoholism is an equal-opportunity disease occurring without regard for gender, race, orientation, education, income, nationality, politics, creed, or code.

PART 1

THE PROBLEM

Jason handed the green and white gravy boat to his wife Lisa, who stood perched atop a red stepladder storing dishes in the kitchen cabinet of their new home in the Plaza Midtown, a high-rise condominium in Atlanta's Midtown. His cell phone chimed, and he retrieved it from his hip. "Hello," he said, "This is Jason Burke."

"Hello, Jason, this is Aaron Middleton," said his caller. "Are you and your new bride settled in yet?"

"Just about," said Jason, looking at Lisa, who gazed down at him quizzically. "We're finishing the unpacking now."

"Progress!" said Middleton, with a smile in his voice. "Is your computer set up?"

Jason thought, *So much for a lazy Sunday evening,* but shot an "OK" sign to Lisa, who smiled and winked at him. Jason wandered out of the kitchen as she climbed down the stepladder to get the few items remaining in the box.

Ten minutes later, as Lisa poured glasses of lemonade, Jason returned, looking vaguely puzzled. "What's the scoop?" she said, passing him his drink.

He took a sip, then smiled and said, "Aaron wants to have breakfast in the morning. He asked me to do a little research tonight."

"On what?"

"The cost of alcoholism to business."

"What for?" Lisa said. "I thought your client was Coyle International Technologies."

"Beats me," Jason said, drinking his lemonade. "Maybe he heard about some of my undergraduate adventures."

"Don't take it so personally," said Lisa. "But why is one of the best consultants in the country interested in drunks?"

"I can't imagine," Jason said. "But you're right: he is one of the best. And people said he has a different approach. The dean told me to keep an open mind."

"Of course."

"I was lucky to get him for a mentor."

"Your GPA had a little to do with that."

"Ah!" said Jason, smiling. "Praise from a veteran consultant!"

"Veteran of a whole year," she laughed.

"So what do you think of this request from my new mentor?"

"I think you'd better get started," she said. "I've got my own clients to see in the morning."

Around 10:30 that night, Jason and Lisa met again in their new kitchen for a cup of chamomile tea, a nightly ritual.

Lisa sipped her tea and said, "Did you find anything interesting?"

Jason had brought with him a yellow legal pad full of notes. He glanced at it, then said, "I felt a little funny when I started. You know, a lot of people drink alcohol—what business is that of Aaron's, or mine? Even if drinking causes problems, isn't it a private matter?"

"That's all true," Lisa nodded. "How many people have problems with alcohol, anyway?"

Jason drank some tea and tapped his notes with his fingertips. "In this country, somewhere between 20 and 30 million."[1]

"Wow," said Lisa softly. "That's around 10 percent of the population."

Jason smiled slightly at his wife's facility with math, and he added: "That includes people with drug addiction."

"Isn't there a difference?"

"Not on the bottom line," said Jason, turning a page in his notes. "The studies I read put the workplace cost of alcoholism between $33 billion and $68 billon every year."[2]

"I had no idea," said Lisa.

"Some studies cite even bigger numbers—losses in productivity, traffic accidents, health-care costs, and more. Alcoholics are absent from work four to eight times more than other employees; and since their drinking affects their families, spouses miss work more often too—wives, husbands, significant others."[3]

"A ripple effect."

Jason nodded. "Alcoholics also have higher rates of accident and injury on the job."

"How dismal does this picture get?" Lisa said.

Jason sipped some more tea and said, "Remember back in business school, we focused on leverage and scalability?"

"Sure."

"OK." Jason turned his notes around and slid them across the table to show Lisa some calculations. Pointing to the numbers, he went ahead: "Studies indicate that at least one in ten Americans is an alcoholic or a drug addict. About 85 percent of these people have jobs."[4]

Lisa looked up at him. "A job masks the problem, doesn't it? It makes them look 'normal.'"

"Right; no one thinks they have a problem because, after all, they're working, aren't they? They are 'functional alcoholics,'" Jason said and pointed to the next figure. "One out of ten may or may not seem high—you can argue it both ways—but the research shows that each alcoholic affects the lives of three or four other people."

"So alcoholism actually affects five people out of ten," said Lisa.

"And those extra people go on and affect even more."

Lisa looked up at Jason. "How many consultants do you think are aware of the extent of this problem?"

"Aaron Middleton makes one," he said. "Now there are at least two more of us."

The next morning, Jason met Aaron at a Waffle House on Peachtree Street. The smell of eggs frying and hash browns on the grill whetted his appetite, and he was glad to see Aaron again. The meeting was their first since Jason had been hired.

"You're right on time," said Aaron rising from his seat in a corner booth and extending his hand. "I like that."

Jason smiled as he shook hands with the older man. "I'm an early riser." He slid onto the opposite bench and reached for a menu.

The waitress brought them two coffees, and, after ordering, they got down to business. Aaron said, with a slight smile, "I doubt you studied anything about alcoholism in business school, did you?"

"No," said Jason, "and I was wondering why you wanted to start with that. Does Coyle International Technologies have a problem with it?"

"I don't know," said Aaron, brightening, "and if they do, they probably don't know either. The issue there is a growing cash-flow problem, even though they have increased revenues 30 percent for three years in a row."

"I guess it is simplistic to say they are spending more than they are making," said Jason

"I suspect there is more to the story than that," said Aaron.

Jason took Aaron's reply as a clue. "You're famous for seeing things that the average consultant misses."

"That's what some people say," Aaron said modestly. "The 'average' guy misses things that I see, in part, because he doesn't look for them." Aaron paused to let this sink in, then enlarged on his theme: "I've learned to look below the surface when I work with a business. I look for the actual causes at the root of a company's difficulties—and find an effective solution, not just a Band-Aid."

"And you think alcoholism lies hidden below the surface."

"Hidden in plain sight," said Aaron. "Based on what you turned up on the Internet last night, how many people does alcoholism affect?"

Jason recalled the exponential effect of alcoholism he had discovered. "Virtually everyone."

"Then, logically, alcoholism also affects every business," said Aaron. "To one degree or another."

Aaron continued: "I don't know a single consultant who looks for alcoholism as an underlying cause of any business problem."

"But you do," said Jason.

"Absolutely."

"Then I assume I'll learn a lot more about the subject."

"Just keep an open mind," Aaron smiled.

As they began to eat, Jason said, "Should I research drug addiction, too?"

"For our purposes," said Aaron, smothering his pecan waffle with syrup, "drug addiction falls under the same umbrella as alcoholism. Prescription drugs, and street drugs like heroin, cocaine, crack, crystal meth—they're all addictive, and they all cause similar damage to that caused by alcoholism. So we'll use the term alcoholism as shorthand for both. And..." he added in a humorous tone, "alcoholism is more acceptable socially."

Over a last cup of coffee, Aaron asked whether Jason felt comfortable with his approach to alcoholism.

"I have just one problem," said Jason. "Various sources refer to alcoholism as a disease. Isn't that just a cop-out for bad behavior? Shouldn't these people be disciplined?"

"Of course, but we don't punish someone for having a disease," said Aaron. "We separate alcoholic behavior from the alcoholic. That's the heart of the approach. It's the various behaviors that need to be addressed. The maladaptive and negative behaviors, and the poor business results following from them, must face direct consequences or they will continue. As consultants, we need to encourage the management of consequences, including good consequences, rewards, for good behavior.

"We'll take all this up again this afternoon. There's a Starbucks across the street from Coyle's offices."

Aaron always knocked off at 4:00, to get out of the client's way while he wrapped up the workday. He and Jason adjourned to the nearby Starbucks. A light crowd sat scattered across the broad dining room, mostly tech types poring over laptops, some housewives finishing a shopping trip, and a few older men in sweaty running togs. Smooth jazz played on the sound system.

Sitting down with a four-shot cappuccino, Jason said, "I've been thinking."

"Good," Aaron smiled over the rim of a large black coffee. A second cup sat at his elbow, still capped.

"I can see the problem of alcoholism on a national scale," said Jason, "but how does it relate to our set of clients?"

"It's hard to see," Aaron nodded. "For twenty-plus years as a consultant, I didn't see it. In fact, practically no one sees it."

Jason frowned. "Not even the alcoholic?"

"Oh, he doesn't see any problem at all with alcohol," Aaron laughed. "He sees problems with unfair competition, or a boss who's a jerk, or the incompetents he has to supervise. Then there's his nagging spouse and the fact that no alcoholic ever has quite the right job. Alcoholism tells the alcoholic he doesn't have a drinking problem."

Jason smiled as Aaron recited this litany of the disease's red herrings.

"The employer's attention also is directed toward all these other 'problems,'" Aaron continued. "And remember, he only sees the alcoholic at work—the tip of the iceberg. Alcoholism affects the totality of a person's life, and all of that has a bearing on what he does at the office. That's the other 90 percent of the iceberg. Alcoholics tend to divert attention from their drinking, whether they are aware of it or not."

"What do we do?" said Jason. "Spy on the employee?"

"Of course not," said Aaron. "We learn to look for the behaviors that are clues to the underlying illness—not alcoholic drinking but its symptoms." Aaron uncapped his other cup of coffee.

"Over the next few days, I'll show you how to identify alcoholism in its early stage, before the average alcoholic even suspects he has a drinking problem. You'll learn how alcoholism works, the stages of its progression, how to identify suspect alcoholics, and then how to respond to it. This awareness will alter how you relate to people in business as well as in your personal life. It may save you great misery someday.

"Think about this: The alcoholic can rarely self-diagnose his disease, especially in the early stages when he's succeeding in business and living the good life in general. The negative consequences haven't begun to accrue yet. The social stigma of alcoholism is fierce and makes all of us wary of suggesting alcoholism as an issue. It's better to call someone crazy than an alcoholic."

"I'm keeping an open mind," Jason said skeptically, "but part of me still says these people just lack character or motivation or discipline."

"Alcoholism is not a lifestyle. It's a disease. Alcoholics don't decide to have alcoholism any more than someone decides to have cancer, diabetes, or any other disease. Once the disease of alcoholism takes hold, the alcoholic has less and less control over his willpower and behavior. He doesn't even know what has happened to him. I don't blame an alcoholic for being sick any more than I blame a person for getting cancer. However, in order to treat the disease, we must hold people directly responsible for their actions and behaviors. The disease concept of alcoholism does not excuse anything," explained Aaron. "Understanding it as a disease allows us to look at it objectively and do something positive about it.

"So tonight, I want you to research the alcoholic's biology. See if you find anything in it that's different from the rest of us."

Jason spent several hours on the Internet that night, reading about the biology of alcoholism. What he found surprised him, as Aaron, no doubt, had known it would.

The body of an alcoholic metabolizes alcohol differently than the body of a normal person. The two drinkers process alcohol differently.

The essence of that difference lies in the speed with which the liver transforms alcohol into two chemicals, first, acetaldehyde, and then, acetate. Acetaldehyde, a toxin, creates the pleasant effect that alcohol has on people. Acetate does the opposite, bringing about sleepiness and nausea. How quickly these processes occur relates directly on the development of alcoholism.

In the normal drinker, alcohol becomes acetaldehyde *slowly*. That drinker enjoys the good feeling of a glass of wine or a scotch on the rocks. Then, the acetaldehyde becomes acetate *quickly*, which he experiences as a sudden sensation of "I've had enough." The toxin, acetaldehyde, does not accumulate in his body or his brain, and has few, if any, harmful effects.

In the alcoholic drinker, the speed of these processes is reversed. His body transforms alcohol into acetaldehyde *rapidly*, with a consequent rush of good feeling. The creation of acetate, on the other hand, occurs *very slowly*. Thus the alcoholic seldom experiences any feeling of having drunk too much, let alone enough. No body or brain signals encourage him to stop. On the contrary, the rapid formation of acetaldehyde sends him a constant message that alcohol makes him feel better and better.

The accumulation of acetaldehyde in the brain triggers a release of "feel-good" neurotransmitters like dopamine that tell the alcoholic drinker he is feeling good. This feeling, in its turn, stimulates even more drinking, and the further build-up of acetaldehyde in the alcoholic's brain.

While he drinks, the accumulation of toxic acetaldehyde actually damages the brain's neocortex, thought to be responsible for reasoning, perception, and logic. Effectively, the poison impairs the alcoholic drinker's perception, judgment, and rational decision-making. The good feeling from acetaldehyde and the 'feel good' neurotransmitters actually prevent awareness of the dangers to which the alcoholic exposes himself by drinking. Rather than a mature and balanced adult perspective, immediate gratification becomes the basis for his action.

The alcoholic drinks alcohol, but eventually it seems that the alcohol itself controls his drinking, through the abnormal metabolic processes accompanying its consumption.

*

*Alcoholism is not in
the bottle—it's in the person.*

*Alcoholism is the only disease you
can get yelled at for having.*

*

"So the alcoholic isn't just a loser, after all," Aaron said to Jason as the Waffle House waitress called out their orders to the multitasking cook. "The biological condition you've learned about may sometimes be an inherited function of genetics. Alcoholism frequently runs in families."

Someone played "Candy Man" on the jukebox, and Aaron winced and shook his head. "There's also accidental addiction: a doctor prescribes a medication and the patient responds to it in a way different from the norm. Then there's the fellow who has a couple of drinks before dinner every night for twenty years. He may develop a dependency on those two drinks. His body adapts and requires those drinks—and more."

Jason turned in his seat and opened his briefcase. "This biological research made me think about the signs of alcoholism at work." He drew out a sheet of paper and laid it on the table facing Aaron, then said, "I found this list at a human resources training site."

Possible Signs of Alcoholism at Work:
1. Frequent tardiness and absences
2. Excuses for missing work and excessive use of sick leave
3. Sloppy work, missed deadlines, declining performance
4. Failure to meet quotas that have been met in the past
5. Strained relationships with coworkers, incessant apologies
6. Shortness of temper, irritability, difficulties in dealing with others
7. Borrowing money from others; asking for advances against payroll
8. Avoidance of certain people, including managers and supervisors
9. Confused thinking and difficulty concentrating
10. Always ready with a good excuse for problems

"Impressive," said Aaron, picking up the printout with a smile. "I'm glad to see you're getting interested."

They talked about the obvious: employees who are hungover, frequently late or plagued by sudden illnesses, those who can barely keep their eyes open, and people whose work has gone from good to bad, neat to sloppy, timely to perpetually late. Then there are those who are always irritable, or always have problems, or avoid other people. The loss of productivity crossed Jason's mind: companies not getting what they pay for from their employees.

Jason went on: "I also remembered a summer internship I did once. One guy was in a fog every morning. All morning. Looking back, I think he was hungover."

"I'll bet he brightened up after lunch," said Aaron, "and I'll bet it was a liquid lunch."

"I hadn't thought of that," he said, a bit chagrined.

Aaron said, "But you had the same experience I've had: Looking back with a new awareness and seeing what very well might have been a symptom of alcoholism. The job is to learn to see the behavioral traits of alcoholism, not just the end results." He tapped the printout with a finger. "This list is a good start, and it could be longer: declining sales, cash-flow problems, increasing debt, potential lawsuits—even criminal behavior." As Aaron spoke, Jason nodded in agreement. "The consultant is told that the problem is cash flow, but it's actually impaired judgment based on distorted perceptions caused by alcoholism. Which is precisely why we want to spot the *potential* alcoholic, long before he exhibits any of these signs and symptoms." Aaron nodded at the printout, then passed it back to Jason as the waitress brought their breakfasts.

"But I'm curious," said Jason. "What can we do about it?"

"The crucial thing at the outset is to remember to target the disease, not the person who has it—a surgically precise approach. But instead of a scalpel, we'll employ consequences—negative consequences following on the heels of the adverse behavior that alcoholism brings out."

"That kind of pain can be a great motivator," said Jason.

*

*The most natural
state of an alcoholic is
restless, irritable,
and discontented.*

*

Aaron asked: "Tell me, Jason, how do you suppose the general public commonly views alcoholism?"

Jason thought for a moment. "They think it's a bad habit. Or that it results from a bad work ethic—poor character, laziness, weak values, the habit of doing the easiest thing rather than the best. Or maybe the alcoholic just lacks the discipline and drive to live right. He could quit if he really wanted to."

"Those are some widely held opinions, all right," Aaron said, shaking his head. "Jason, we need to remember that people don't choose their diseases. True, to a great degree we choose our lifestyles, but as I've said, alcoholism isn't a lifestyle. It's a disease that erodes willpower, distorts perceptions, and impairs judgment. After decades of research and debate, the evidence points overwhelmingly to this conclusion.

"There are other approaches as well, such as the psychological, or mental, model of alcoholism. According to that model, alcoholic drinking results from dire circumstances. But if that were true, then once the circumstances change, or the individual responds to them differently, he should be able to return to healthy social drinking. In thousands of studies, that hasn't been the finding.

"No, the evidence, and the conclusions of the vast majority of researchers, deems alcoholism a disease," Aaron concluded. "And it's a progressive disease. The common, widely known signs of alcoholism don't usually show up until the disease is well-advanced, but I'll show you how to spot the early indicators. These indicators don't prove alcoholism, but they do serve as red flags to alert our attention. That's critical in protecting ourselves and our businesses from damage caused by alcoholism."

"You seem to think there's a lot more to alcoholism than meets the eye," Jason said.

"You bet! The magnitude of the problem is enormous. What's strange is that the very same traits that help many individuals and businesses to succeed spring from alcoholism. But as alcoholism progresses, alcoholic behavior changes in increasingly negative ways, while alcohol as the cause is less and less obvious," Aaron said.

"The real danger is that alcoholic behavior and addictive thinking continue whether the alcoholic is drinking or not. We usually think of alcoholism in terms of the drunk driver, a barroom brawl, or the sloppy drunk, but alcoholics often form a bigger threat after the alcohol wears off. An alcoholic is damaged goods, whether he's drinking or not. When he isn't drinking, our guard is down, and the chance for greater damage increases," Aaron went on. "It's alcoholic behavior and alcoholic thinking that hurt a business, not the fact of drinking. It's by their behaviors that you'll learn to identify alcoholics early. This puts you in a position to protect yourself and a business before the damage occurs.

"Behavior," Aaron said again. "That's the key to alcoholism's effect on business—not the fact of being an alcoholic, but what the alcoholic does, whether obvious or not. Alcoholic behaviors harm employees, finances, and relationships with coworkers, customers, vendors, and many others. Owners and executives need to understand these behaviors as threats to their company. None of us can see the disease, but we all can see the behavior."

"But what if the owners or executives are the alcoholics?" said Jason.

"Then knowledgeable employees need to be alert to erratic behavior that may affect them," said Aaron, "like firings without genuine cause, or cash-flow problems, or the boss running the company into the ground while everyone loses their job."

"Okay, here's a messy one: what if our client is the alcoholic?" Jason asked. "We do want to get paid, don't we?"

"That's one of the issues we'll be looking at in the next few weeks. I'm glad you're thinking forward. Keep your eyes and ears open, and most importantly, your mind." Aaron looked at his wristwatch, then said, "That's all the time we've got for this morning. Let's head over to Coyle's and pick this up again at Starbucks this afternoon."

*

*Being an
alcoholic does
not give anyone
the excuse to
act alcoholically.*

*

Coyle Technologies had an executive staff meeting at 3:00, so Aaron and Jason adjourned to the local Starbucks earlier than they had planned. As Jason took his seat across from Aaron, he noticed a tall attractive blonde walking toward their table.

"Hi, Patricia," Aaron smiled up at the young woman. "It's good to see you. Allow me to introduce Jason Burke, a fresh B-school grad who's working with me this year. Have a seat, I'm going to get a Danish." Aaron rose and looked at the others. "Can I get you anything?"

Patricia and Jason passed on any snacks, and Aaron crossed to the counter.

"Nice to meet you," Patricia said to Jason as she sat down. "I thought I might run into Aaron here. About this time last year, I was the new consultant mentoring with him."

"And how was it?" Jason said.

"Amazing," Patricia replied. "You'll build on what you learned at school in very practical ways. Has he started talking about alcoholism yet?"

"He started the night before my first day," Jason laughed.

"You'll think that Aaron believes everything relates to alcoholism," she said. "Of course, he knows it doesn't, but it seems that way at first because it's such a new angle on business problems."

"He does seem obsessed with it," said Jason, "but I trust he has a point to make."

"Let me tell you something I learned from Aaron," said Patricia. "First, alcoholism's stigma and the lack of understanding about it make it difficult to identify as the cause of many problems. Most people still believe that alcoholism results from a character weakness.

"From Aaron, I learned that considering the possibility of alcoholism actually gives the troubled employee a break. If he has alcoholism, he has a solution available. Otherwise, he's just a bad apple, or a weak character, or lacking in competence."

Aaron came back with a cheese Danish.

Patricia's face brightened as Aaron returned. "I just gave Jason the bottom line on alcoholism," she said to him. Then she clutched her purse and rose from the table. "I need to get my coffee and head out," she said. "Fasten your seatbelt, Jason. Your perspective on many business problems is about to change completely."

As Patricia crossed to the counter to order, Jason turned to his mentor and asked: "Aaron, doesn't investigating the possibility of alcoholism raise privacy issues?"

"The disease does raise those issues, since drinking on the job is rare," Aaron replied. "That's why we'll focus on alcoholic behaviors, not alcoholic drinking. The stigma of alcoholism discourages people from acting or even talking openly. And alcoholics don't seem to act until they reach a point of desperation, helplessness, and pain."

"You asked me to keep an open mind, and I will," said Jason, "but we certainly didn't spend time on this at business school."

"I've seen much personal and professional tragedy as a result of alcoholism," Aaron replied. "And it goes even deeper than that. Usually, we think about the consequences of our actions. This is different. We must think about the consequences of doing nothing. As you'll see, with alcoholism and addiction, the odds are overwhelming that the user will crash and burn, physically, emotionally, and financially. Or they may just find a way to get by and live a miserable, unfulfilled, depressing existence. A life of missed opportunity. If a person is our friend or coworker, why do we simply abandon him to such destruction?

"Alcoholics have to hit bottom to change. For too many, that bottom is death. The key is to find ways to raise the bottom, to let the pain hit sooner, to force the decision earlier."

"What's a 'bottom'? I hear that phrase, and I want to understand it," Jason said.

"Before we go there, I want you to look up some of the definitions of alcoholism on the Internet," Aaron said. "Print them out and let's look at them in the morning. Before we can get into identifying early-stage alcoholics, we need some common understanding about accepted knowledge and science."

"Will do," Jason said.

"Good morning, Jason," Aaron said as they settled into their usual booth at the Waffle House. "Did you find any definitions of alcoholism last night?"

"I sure did," Jason said. "I read quite a bit on a number of medical and governmental Web sites. The damage done to the alcoholic's brain impressed me the most—maybe that's why I say some of my boozing friends are brain-dead."

"The neocortical damage is significant and serious," Aaron nodded. "I'm not a neurosurgeon, of course, but it's worth noting this scientific explanation for alcoholic behavior. The distorted perceptions and impaired judgment stemming from that damage make alcoholics a risk to any business. The important point is that this impairment remains even when the alcoholic isn't drinking. The alcoholic is damaged goods. The questions are: how damaged is he, and how much damage can he still inflict on others?"

Jason spoke up. "It reminds me of what Einstein said, 'The level of thinking that causes the problem cannot solve the problem.'"

"That's a good point," Aaron replied. "The big problem is, alcoholics don't take themselves down alone, they pull others down with them."

"I found several definitions of alcoholism," said Jason. "As you asked, I considered the sources, what they had in common, and what was different. There wasn't a universally agreed-upon definition, but I've printed out a couple that seem comprehensive and authoritative."

> In 1990, the Board of Directors of the National Council on Alcoholism and Drug Dependence and the American Society of Addiction Medicine, approved the following definition:
>
> *Alcoholism is a primary, chronic disease with genetic, psychosocial, and environmental factors influencing its development and manifestations. The disease is often progressive and fatal. It is characterized by continuous or periodic: impaired control over drinking, preoccupation with the drug alcohol, use of alcohol despite adverse consequences, and distortions in thinking, most notably denial.*

"That's interesting, but we know more now," Aaron said. "The earliest definitions of alcoholism only described the later stages of the disease. Most definitions fail to recognize the earlier stages.

"Many early-and middle-stage alcoholics enjoy their drinking much of the time. The point is that the disease progresses: with time, the alcoholic's drinking becomes less pleasant and increasingly destructive. That progression is what we want to stop," he said.

"Here's another definition from a medical site," Jason said.

Below are the criteria of the American Psychiatric Association in their Diagnostic and Statistical manual (DSM-IV). In this definition, an alcoholic must show three or more of the following symptoms within a twelve-month period.

1. Tolerance, defined as a need for increasingly larger amounts of alcohol to achieve intoxication (over time the drug produces less intense reactions at the same dose).
2. Withdrawal symptoms, which include hand tremor, sweating, elevated pulse rate, insomnia, nausea, or anxiety; these symptoms may develop into hallucinations, grand mal seizures, and/or psychotic symptoms.
3. Drinking in larger amounts over longer periods than intended.
4. Persistent desire or unsuccessful attempts to cut down or control drinking.
5. Spending a significant amount of time trying to obtain alcohol, drink alcohol, or recover from its effects.
6. Giving up social, occupational, or recreational activities because of alcohol.
7. Continuing to drink despite persistent or recurrent physical or psychological problems caused or exacerbated by alcohol use.

"I hoped you'd find these two definitions," said Aaron. "But there are two others that better capture the nature of the disease. Katherine Ketchum, a leading authority on the disease, bases this definition on more current research." Aaron handed Jason a printout.

> *Alcoholism is a progressive neurological disease strongly influenced by genetic vulnerability. Inherited or acquired abnormalities in brain chemistry create an altered response to alcohol that in turn causes a wide array of physical, psychological, and behavioral problems. Although environmental and social factors will influence the progress and express of the disease, they are not in any sense causes of addictive drinking.*
>
> *Alcoholism is caused by biochemical/neurophysiological abnormalities that are passed down from one generation to the next or, in some cases acquired through heavy or prolonged drinking[5].*

"And here's another definition," Aaron said, passing Jason a second page. "Alcoholism researcher and author Doug Thorburn lays the issue out very simply."

> *Alcoholism is a genetic disorder that causes the afflicted to biochemically process the drug alcohol in such a way as to cause that person to engage in destructive behaviors, at least some of the time[6].*

"Thorburn's definition," Aaron said, "stresses the loss of control and destructive behavior that alcoholics experience—something that a lot of other researchers don't necessarily emphasize.

"Ketchum's and Thorburn's definitions each suggest that we view dysfunctional behaviors as clues to early-stage alcoholism. These behavioral signs allow us to identify the disease before it becomes obvious. If we can identify early-stage alcoholism and act proactively, we can protect our clients from the alcoholic's destructive behavior and avoid a lot of trouble. Otherwise, we're just waiting for a disaster to happen—and when it does, we wonder *Why?*"

Aaron concluded: "If alcohol causes repeated problems for an employee, and he still doesn't stop drinking, isn't that a sign that he may have the disease of alcoholism? An alcoholic will continue to drink even when negative consequences, common sense and logic all tell him to stop. He may have accidents, DUIs, family fights, financial

*

*To an alcoholic, an alcoholic
is anyone he doesn't like who
drinks more than he does.*

*

trouble, and lost jobs, but he can continue to rationalize his drinking, in spite of it all. Alcoholism isn't determined by how much a person drinks, but by what happens when he does drink."

As Aaron paused, Jason added, "It still bothers me that alcoholics can hide behind the disease concept as an excuse for their bad behavior."

"Many people, hearing alcoholism described as a disease, assume that makes it a license to escape the consequences of drunken behavior. Whether the alcoholic is truly responsible for what he does under the influence is a question for ethics, but the truth is that virtually all alcoholics feel guilt over their behavior while drinking, and even about the drinking itself. So taking responsibility for that behavior—altering his thinking, changing the way he thinks about and treats others, and, most important, making amends to whomever he has hurt—all become vitally important to recovery from alcoholism.

"After all," Aaron leaned forward a bit to emphasize his point, "doesn't an alcoholic drink if he feels guilty?" He sat back in his chair as Jason nodded. "So he needs to dispel those guilt feelings. In the overwhelming majority of recovering alcoholics, the mere idea of the disease concept of alcoholism does not truly relieve the pain of their past. That can only be accomplished through genuine character reform. The disease concept of alcoholism opens the door to treatments that include that kind of moral undertaking."

Aaron sipped his coffee. "Of course," he went on, "some people who have been hurt by an alcoholic resent the idea that their abuser 'suffers from a disease.' They need to understand that responsibility and accountability are critical to the healing of the alcoholic.

"The picture is complicated by the unfortunate fact that many people, including a lot of employers, unintentionally enable the alcoholic by *not* holding him accountable and refusing to enforce consequences for unacceptable behavior. They 'go easy' on the guy out of a misplaced sense of forgiveness. You can't 'forgive' a disease—or 'punish' it. It's the alcoholic's behavior that does the damage, directly and indirectly, so that has to change. The alcoholic has to accept the consequences of his own acts, drunk or sober. That makes him responsible—for recovering.

"The alcoholic must arrest his illness and get well. Of course, at the outset, he doesn't want to get well. He just wants things to settle down and become 'normal,' whatever that means to him. But if he stays sober, he comes to desire wellness. The disease is progressive, but fortunately, so is recovery. The goals of the recovering alcoholic change and grow the longer he stays sober."

"You've mentioned progression several times," said Jason. "Could you describe that a little more?"

Aaron looked at his watch. "It's almost time to wrap up for the day," he said. "But in a nutshell: alcoholism progresses at different rates in different people. It can be like cancer, sometimes very aggressive and other times slow-growing. *But it always progresses.* The best the alcoholic can do is stop the drinking, which allows him to restore mental and physical health. Let me emphasize that this requires *total abstinence*—absolutely no alcohol, not even a sip of wine. Even that much can make the brain scream for more and start the whole vicious cycle all over again."

Jason decided to try to get ahead of Aaron. *After all,* he thought, *it always helps to make a good impression.* Driving home, he thought again about the progressive nature of alcoholism. *It isn't like a light bulb, all bright one minute and burned out the next.* The disease advances through stages, much like a cancer. With alcoholism, there are early, middle, and late stages, although symptoms may overlap from one stage to the next. Aaron repeatedly stressed this progression, and, with it, the alcoholic's only hope: to arrest the disease by stopping drinking alcohol altogether. *If it's a disease,* thought Jason with a sudden chill, *it's an incurable disease.*

Jason wanted Aaron to discuss the progressive stages at their next meeting and did his own research before they met. He went by a bookstore to check over some books on the subject. Several discussed the stages of the disease. *Beyond the Influence*[7] by Katherine Ketchum impressed him the most. Other books said much the same as Ketchum's: alcoholism progresses through stages—early, middle, and late—and the characteristics of each stage may carry over into the others.

His reading increased his appreciation for the complexity of alcoholism. Descriptions of the disease's progression detailed the changes in the alcoholic's behavior with time. *The same disease causes opposite behaviors in the same person, depending on the stage*, Jason thought.

All the books identified, more or less, the same stages. In the early stage, the alcoholic has no sense of a problem, mainly because his tolerance for alcohol is increasing, and he doesn't get drunk very easily. As the old saying goes, he "can hold his liquor."

Basic signs of alcoholism in the early stage include:

- An intense pleasure associated with drinking
- A high tolerance for alcohol and its effects
- A consequent preoccupation with drinking alcohol

Early-stage alcoholism hides from most of us, including the alcoholic. In this stage, also called *the adaptive stage*, the body undergoes physical adaptations to alcohol. The alcoholic's gradually increasing tolerance encourages increased consumption of alcohol, which has fewer effects—a subtle and usually unnoticed progression.

The body and brain of the early-stage alcoholic adapt to his condition by increasing their tolerance for alcohol. He never knows he has "had enough," let alone that he needs to stop. Physical changes occur in the alcoholic's nervous system that can lead to an actual improvement of functioning when he is under the influence. Thus, the early-stage alcoholic functions at a high level. Alcoholics in this stage suffer fewer side effects from drinking than most normal drinkers, who have to stop after a few drinks.

The positive effects of alcohol at the early stage—warmth, openness, a feeling of really being alive—naturally result in the development by the alcoholic to a preoccupation with drinking. Why not look forward to more of this boon to mankind? The preoccupation can take subtle forms, such as a mid-afternoon anticipation of happy hour, planning events around drinking, or just sprinkling conversation with talk of cocktails or the latest California wine.

The good feelings and overall positive attitudes that characterize the early stage interfere with any sense of the emerging problem on the part of the alcoholic or his friends and associates. Drinking alcohol makes him feel good, and better than good. He has a better mood, experiences less tension, and has an improved sense of well-being and confidence. The alcoholic would have to deny his own senses to entertain any opinion of alcohol other than that its effects on him are tonic, heightening his experience of life and reducing his level of stress. Alcohol naturally becomes an important part of his life. He will ensure that it is always readily available. Alcohol is his friend, and cannot be his enemy. He *deserves* a drink today.

No clear line marks the boundary between the early and middle stages of alcoholism, and some traits of the disease can occur in both stages. Rather than strictly delimiting the phases of alcoholism, the concept of stages aids in describing the progressive nature of the disease, and the behavioral changes that advance as drinking continues. The alcoholic remains unaware of his newly acquired physical dependence on alcohol, which began in the early stage.

By the middle stage, some of the destructive aspects of alcoholic drinking begin to displace many of its previous pleasures. The inevitable downslide becomes observable, though the cause, excessive drinking, may still remain unrecognized by the alcoholic and others. Drinking for pleasure becomes a receding memory, slowly but unavoidably replaced by drinking to reduce the stress of troubles and cares, which are themselves often brought on by prior drinking.

Basic signs of middle-stage alcoholism are:
- Social withdrawal
- Blackouts—episodes of amnesia induced by drinking
- Personality disintegration
- Denial

Physical dependence and cravings for alcohol characterize the middle stage. The alcoholic's tolerance has increased and he gradually loses his ability to control his consumption. Physical cravings and obsessive thinking about having a drink become a seemingly natural part of his life. His loss of control begins to become obvious to other people. If he grows self-conscious—for instance, after someone says something about his drinking—he begins to drink in private, away from the people who know him. He falls into the repetitive pattern of having "Just one more drink before I stop."

He still feels good when he drinks, but life in general is not quite what it used to be, neither as simple nor as easy as it seemed in the past. Difficulties such as moodiness and depression seem, to the alcoholic, to be brought on by "other people"—complainers, children, bosses, spouses or lovers, or people interfering with the control of his money. The continually anticipated "good time" of drinking gradually fades away.

Such impairments are obvious to some people, but the majority do not notice them unless they know what to look for. At work, the alcoholic is late more and has more unplanned absences. His performance declines and disagreements with coworkers increase. He seems to be in a fog, without his former ability to concentrate. Accidents befall him regularly, with resultant scrapes on his hands and knees, pulled muscles, and endless new aches and pains.

Should the middle-stage alcoholic take a break from drinking, he experiences anxiety, irritability, nervousness, impulsiveness, difficulty sleeping, and even more changes. In fact, his body is undergoing an alcoholic withdrawal from drinking. Other people rarely associate these symptoms with alcohol.

Blackouts are a commonly accepted symptom of middle-stage alcoholism, although they can occur in the early stage as well. A blackout is not an episode of "passing out" or other form of unconsciousness. The alcoholic functions fairly normally in a blackout, but cannot later recall what he did or where he went. His brain does not store or cannot retrieve these memories. In fact, the alcoholic may not even be aware he has had a blackout until someone else mentions something that occurred while he was in this eerie netherworld. Such incidents—the inability to recall how he got home, or what happened after a certain point of the evening—are clear danger signs of the progression of the disease.

While in a blackout, the alcoholic may appear to function normally. This is possible because his tolerance is so high. He can pursue work and other everyday activities—performing surgery, flying an airplane, painting a house, participating in a meeting, driving a car, or having a conversation—but he will have no recollection afterward of anything that occurred during the blackout.

A blackout can be triggered by as little as a few sips of alcohol. Heavy drinking is not required to bring it on.

In middle stage, the alcoholic begins to rationalize any suspicions he has that he might be an alcoholic. He thinks he is different from "those drunks"—the ones who lack character and discipline, the physically unfit, the mental cases, and the bums. He relies on the presence of certain externals—job, car, spouse, family, house and other possessions—to argue that his internal problem, alcoholism, does not exist. He says to himself and to others:

- "Alcoholism runs in families—it's inherited—and it isn't in my family, so I'm safe."
- "I'm a success! I make more money than I need! I can't be an alcoholic!"
- "I only drink beer and wine, and if I do get drunk, it's only on a weekend."
- "I'm nowhere near as bad as my friends."

The alcoholic will not let anyone or anything interfere with his established drinking routines. He reacts to any interference with or comments about his drinking with annoyance and resentment. The claim that he can "handle" his drinking, and that others should "mind their own business," are typical responses. Delusions and denials have become a way of life.

By the late stage, the alcoholic's plight becomes obvious to even the most casual observer, though the drinker himself may still remain unaware. He is irrational, deluded, and unable to comprehend why his life has fallen apart. Major health problems are blatantly evident.

He is typically broke and possibly homeless, suffering from multiple illnesses and a permanent fog of mental confusion. He drinks almost constantly. Common medical conditions of the late stage include hepatitis, cirrhosis of the liver, malnutrition, pancreatitis, respiratory infections, heart failure, and brain damage. He is headed for an early death. If steps are taken to stop his drinking, some of the damage done to his health may be reversible.

*

In the beginning,
the alcoholic takes a drink,
the drink takes a drink,
and then drink takes the alcoholic.

Alcoholism is like
holding a hand grenade
without a pin.

Alcoholism is
a disease of denial.

*

The Waffle House was more crowded than usual, and Aaron and Jason had to wait a few minutes for a table.

"Morning," said Jason as they stood together beside the jukebox. "I went by the bookstore again last night to read some more about the stages of alcoholism."

"It's good to see you put in the extra time," said Aaron with an appreciative smile. "Now that we've covered the progressive stages of alcoholism, I'm going to show you how to identify alcoholics early on."

"From what I read," said Jason, "I don't see how it can be recognized in the early stage."

"It's not, unless you know what to look for," said Aaron. Two construction workers got up from the booth in the far corner, and Aaron and Jason made a beeline for it.

After they ordered, Aaron turned back to his perennial subject. "Two phenomena occur commonly among alcoholics in each of the stages—*denial* and *rationalization*," he said. "As you begin to understand how the alcoholic mind works and what addictive thinking really is, you'll see the potential dangers to business of each of these mental twists. Awareness is key to protect ourselves and our clients."

"It's a matter of looking for the known clues," Jason nodded.

"You frequently hear the word *denial* in talk of alcoholism. Denial is very important, but largely misunderstood. You can't actually deny something when you aren't aware of it, and the alcoholic, remember, is unaware of his problem. The word *denial* suggests the intent to hide something or to not admit it. The alcoholic cannot formally deny his alcoholism because he doesn't know that he has it. His problem, should you ask him, is all these circumstances and these 'other people.' As you'll see, the alcoholic's suffering is compounded by these self-favoring distortions of perception and memory.

*

DENIAL = Don't Even Know I Am Lying

*

"But avoiding awareness of an issue is also a form of denial. Avoiding the awareness that his life is crumbling, that things just are not working out, that he is growing increasingly isolated from others and the world, that he is falling into debt—this sort of avoidance is what we mean by alcoholic denial. He refuses to recognize his circumstances." Aaron sipped his coffee and continued. "So denial isn't lying. The alcoholic in a state of denial actually believes his distorted construction of reality."

"Fascinating," said Jason. "He really is mentally ill."

"Exactly. Sometimes the alcoholic will 'go on the wagon,' drinking less or even stopping altogether for a while, to deceive himself that this capacity to 'moderate' proves he is not an alcoholic. Of course, he announces his temporary temperance to his friends and associates, to let them know, should they suspect he has a problem with alcohol, that he 'can take it or leave it alone.' But here is the catch: Who has to prove they *don't* have a problem? Normal drinkers don't worry about having a drinking problem, let alone try to establish that they don't. The idea simply doesn't cross their minds."

"That's really interesting," said Jason. "I always assumed that denial was an expressed denial by the alcoholic that he has a drinking problem. But denial of the circumstances of alcoholism is just as necessary to the progression of the disease."

"The fundamental move is the alcoholic's denial that his life is becoming *unmanageable*," said Aaron. "That denial avoids an awareness that is essential to recovery—so the alcoholic must explain it away in order to continue his alcoholic drinking. The recognition and admission of anything that interferes with drinking generates a defensive rationalization in the alcoholic mind."

"So denial and rationalization actually work together?" Jason asked.

"Precisely," Aaron nodded. "A rationalization is the 'good reason' instead of the true reason. When we rationalize, we offer a distraction from the truth, the real causes of whatever we are explaining away. When we rationalize we tell 'rational lies.'"

"Clever," Jason smiled.

"Rationalization makes it unnecessary for us to face the truth," said Aaron. "It certainly makes it hard to correct a problem when we won't even look at the facts. Failure to recognize problems results in self-defeating behavior.

"Rationalization begins internally. We first convince ourselves of our hollow reasoning. We all know people who 'believe their own BS,'" said Aaron. "They're not aware of rationalizing anything.

"Remember what you read about the damage alcoholism does to the neocortex—the perception and judgment area of the brain? If someone wants to do something bad enough, any rationalization will do the trick. We've all been in situations where someone acted ridiculously or perhaps even criminally, but sincerely believed their behavior made perfect sense."

"Sure," said Jason.

*

Rationalization is an intellectually respectable, ego-serving excuse for doing things I had no business doing.

*

"This takes us to an interesting area rarely discussed," said Aaron. "The mind of the alcoholic." He drew closer to the table and went on. "I've read extensively in this area, and I think alcoholism researcher Doug Thorburn has drawn the best distinctions about the alcoholic mind. At any rate, his points confirm my experience completely. Here's what Doug says:

"A critical distortion in the alcoholic brain is the inability to perceive and judge accurately. This defect underlies the distortions in the alcoholic's perception and memory. 'Euphoric recall,' for instance, occurs when the alcoholic remembers what he experienced or did while drinking as good, right, and positive, with little or nothing on the negative end of the spectrum. Remember that phrase—*euphoric recall*—because this phenomenon will help later when we talk about the identifying clues to alcoholism."[8]

Jason made a note of it.

"A trait well known among people who have studied alcoholism is the alcoholic's 'inflated ego.' We hear a lot about 'ego-inflating behaviors' and 'bloated self-importance,'" said Aaron.

"According to Thorburn, an early-stage alcoholic resorts to three common behaviors to 'inflate' his ego. First, he compulsively wields power over others—this satisfies his need to dominate, to have the last word. Second, he acts recklessly, which shows what he can get away with because he is different from the rest of us—his case is 'special.'

Third, and this surprises just about everyone, he overachieves," said Aaron.

"I've never connected overachievement with alcoholism," said Jason.

"Exactly," said Aaron. "Overachievement is the grand paradox of alcoholism. The stereotypical alcoholic is a bum, a man or woman on their way down and out. But remember what characterized early-stage alcoholism: the alcoholic who tolerates alcohol well and appears to be 'functional' is likely to be above average in many areas, and may even succeed fabulously. Watch out for this guy—he's in a position to cause the most harm in business since no one suspects he has any 'issues.' And his previous success overshadows any current screw-ups or misbehaviors, so he tends to be shielded from negative consequences. The typical response is: 'Oh, that's so out of character.'

"As you can tell from all the foregoing, the big problem with early-stage alcoholism is that you don't see it unless you're actively looking for it," said Aaron.

"But since the disease is progressive," Jason speculated aloud, "it seems the poor performance and maladaptive behaviors become obvious later."

"Exactly," Aaron replied. "The challenge is to identify alcoholics early and protect ourselves and our clients before the serious trouble really begins. I'm going to show you how to spot the signs and behaviors that appear long before the excessive drinking becomes a known issue."

PART 2:

IDENTIFYING THE SIGNS OF ALCOHOLISM

"During our next few meetings, I'll show you some of the signs that help identify likely alcoholics. The display of these symptoms doesn't mean that the person definitely has the disease. Rather, these red flags increase the probability that the individual has alcoholism. Remember that probability isn't proof," Aaron cautioned. "We're looking for early indicators so we can build in protections for ourselves and our work."

"It does sound kind of like a witch hunt," Jason said.

"I understand your concern," said Aaron. "This information can be misused, though that's certainly not my intention. My purpose is education—to foster a general knowledge of the problem. With the potential of alcoholism to damage a business enterprise, people need such awareness and information to take certain steps *before they are needed*. By being alert and cautious, we increase the chances of avoiding disaster."

Jason nodded, saying, "And since alcoholism is a progressive disease, the earlier the alcoholic is encouraged, or even required, to seek help, the greater the benefit to everyone."

"The first red flag is family history," said Aaron. "A person with alcoholism in his family has a four to seven times greater chance of having alcoholism than someone without such a background. Family history doesn't make alcoholism a certainty—siblings of an alcoholic may not necessarily be alcoholic themselves. But let's be realistic: all by itself, alcoholism in someone's family history should be a heads-up."

"That makes sense," Jason agreed. "All the definitions emphasize a genetic predisposition to the disease. Diseases like breast cancer, heart disease, and sickle cell anemia all run in families, so why not alcoholism?"

"Remember, though," Aaron cautioned, "the tentative nature of these signs and symptoms. They all *suggest* the possibility of alcoholism. They don't *prove* it."

"Of course not," said Jason.

"Another early telltale sign is the drinker who gulps his first few drinks," Aaron went on. "He is ordering his second drink while his friends or coworkers have barely touched their first ones. He'll also drink shots with a beer, a habit that quickly elevates his blood-alcohol level. I knew one fellow who always ordered a shot of Jack Daniels with a beer while he waited for his coworkers to meet him for drinks after work. That way he hid his excessive drinking. At any rate, he thought he did—the empty shot glasses lined up on the bar usually gave him away."

Aaron smiled as Jason shook his head, then continued. "There's also 'pre-drinking,'" he said. "That's having some stiff drinks at home or in the privacy of the office before going out to meet friends. This technique enables the alcoholic to appear to drink in a 'normal' way when he connects with his friends. And he can drink faster than the nonalcoholic because of his higher tolerance. He's just beginning to feel the buzz when others are ready to stop."

"As you said the other day," Jason commented, "the alcoholic processes the alcohol differently from the rest of us, and that contributes to his higher tolerance for it."

"Hey!" Aaron smiled brightly and pointed at Jason. "You're connecting the dots!"

"Okay," Jason laughed. "Now give me one that'll surprise me."

"How about cigarette smoking?" said Aaron.

"Are you serious?" said Jason.

"Smoking is a major indicator of possible alcoholism," Aaron nodded. "Smokers have a three to five times greater probability than non-smokers of having alcoholism.[9]

"Again, not every smoker is an alcoholic," Aaron cautioned. "On the other hand, most alcoholics are smokers. Smoking is bad for your health, but at least it doesn't distort your perception and warp your behavior. About 25 percent of Americans smoke, but among alcoholics, 80 to 90 percent are cigarette smokers. There seems to be some genetic connection.

"So we can use smoking as a red flag for potential alcoholism," Aaron continued. "According to a recent Yale study[10], non-daily smokers are five times more likely to abuse alcohol, and pack-a-day smokers are three times as likely. Any smoker, even the occasional one who 'just smokes when he has a drink,' flies a red flag as far as we're concerned. Another analysis of the data shows that one in three smokers has alcoholism.[11] Smoking doesn't prove alcoholism, let alone cause it, but experts consider it a high probability indicator."

"You aren't declaring war on smoking, are you?" said Jason.

"No, though maybe we should. I'm just pointing out indicators of increased likelihood of alcoholism. This indicator—cigarette smoking—appears in the behavior even before the drinker is consuming to excess."

Jason shook his head, a little overwhelmed. "It's amazing to me that all these physical signs occur, as it were, 'around' alcoholism and the alcoholic's history and behavior."

"There's a constellation of factors and signs of the disease," said Aaron. "One of the outstanding ones is the alcoholic's obsession with drinking.

"A drink is frequently on his mind, even at the earliest stages," he said. "He always finds a way to make drinking an acceptable, ordinary part of life and work. He likes to have a drink after work, when he talks something over, or just to unwind. Problems resolve easily under the spell of alcohol. His obsession can be very subtle, but you will often hear him counting down to Happy Hour in the middle of the afternoon: 'Three more hours to a cocktail,' he'll say, or 'Man! I really need a drink after that phone call.' He isn't even aware of his obsession, but it's obvious if you pay attention."

"I saw that today at Coyle's," said Jason. "A lot of the sales department's activities revolve around drinking. Having a drink comes up again and again in their conversations. The sales manager wants to drink to celebrate everything. Meeting their weekly goal was today's occasion. He shouted out: 'Drinks on the company,' but it seemed to me that most of the staff would rather have gotten the money and gone home."

"Sure," said Aaron. "That's a nice way to keep drinking an acceptable part of work, not to mention justifying his drinking to himself and the others as part of the job."

"Drinking is never inappropriate to someone with alcoholism," said Jason.

"It can't be," said Aaron. "We've been talking about some of the physical signs—specific observable things that may indicate an increased probability of alcoholism. Next, I want to talk about something more subtle, but just as apparent once you know what to look for: behavioral signs."

NOTES OF PHYSICAL SIGNS
- Family history
- Gulps drinks, does shots, pre-drinks
- Smokes
- Mental obsession

"Just as the stages of alcoholism progression overlap, the clues to the behavior at each stage also overlap," explained Aaron. "The clues to alcoholism remain valid, regardless of the stage in which they exhibit themselves. They still indicate alcoholism.

"Here are some clues to alcoholism that researcher and author Doug Thorburn has identified," said Aaron, passing a printout across the table at Starbucks.

> In early stage, the person has 1) a "Supreme being" complex and 2) shows signs of a sense of invincibility. These are driven by the alcoholic's need to inflate his ego and is evident by ego-inflating behaviors.
>
> In middle stage, as the disease progresses, the alcoholic 3) shows repeated poor judgment and 4) signs of mental confusion. The destructive behaviors accelerate with the poor judgment and mental confusion (also in late stage).[12]

When Jason finished reading, Aaron continued: "In the late stage, the physical signs and lack of mental capacity become blatant.

"One of the main problems with recognizing alcoholism at the early stage is that the negative effects of the disease remain unnoticeable. The alcoholic has a preoccupation with drinking, but it's rare for anyone to be aware of it. Destructive behaviors are just beginning to appear, and even then, the alcoholic exhibits them only from time to time.

"But they can be seen if you look for them. Once you know them, the behaviors of early alcoholism start to become clear long before the onset of destructive behavior.

"One simple fact stands out glaringly: an alcoholic's distorted perception leads to impaired judgment, which, in turn, results in bad choices and negative, maladaptive behaviors.

"Remember alcoholism's grand paradox?" said Aaron. "Alcoholics frequently attain significant achievements during the early stage. Alcoholism causes egomania. You'll sometimes hear a recovering alcoholic say that he was 'an egomaniac with an inferiority complex.' That is, the extreme egotist over-compensates for his truly low self-esteem. He is driven to display a high level of competence and productivity in order to inflate his ego.

"Of course, all high performers are not alcoholics, but it is one of the clues, particularly when it appears in combination with other clues.

"Performance can actually improve in the early stage as the alcoholic's ambition and ego-inflating forces combine. The need to compensate leads to increasing competencies and a drive to outperform others. The high level of achievement conceals the alcoholic's low self-esteem and, with it, the disease. This all occurs in the early stage, remember, so you won't see it unless you look for it."

Aaron went on. "The danger to a business lies in the alcoholic's need to win at any cost, even at the expense of other people and of the truth. The institutionalized protection generally given to high achievers only adds to the problem by allowing them to operate by their own separate set of rules.

"The higher the professional status, the greater this sort of built-in enabling. Executives, doctors, attorneys, athletes, entertainers, and politicians—all stand at increased risk of such enabling.

"People protect alcoholics if they have something to lose should the alcoholic suffer and fall. From such self-interest, coworkers and subordinates shield the alcoholic, defend him, cover up for him, or look away from his problems," Aaron said.

"A 'stress junkie' may be, in fact, an early-stage alcoholic," he continued. "A stress, or crisis junkie thrives on chaos. What better way for the damaged ego to inflate itself, perhaps unconsciously, than to create a crisis and then resolve the dire situation. 'Saved the day again!' the stress junkie declares, if only to himself.

"I had one client who was fond of announcing projects to workers the day before or even the day of a deadline, though he knew about them days or weeks in advance. This guy is also prone to loud office rants and rages, which earn him a dominating big-dog position."

"I know guys like that," Jason said.

"So do I," said Aaron. "Almost everyone does."

Aaron ordered another black coffee and brought it back to the table. Then he went on: "People who are predisposed to alcoholism start thinking at a very early age about occupations that will inflate and flatter their egotism. They don't realize what they're doing. Most alcoholics have their first drinks between the ages of 13 and 15.[13] They aren't drinking to excess yet, but alcoholic thought processes are emerging. They already have an inflated sense of their importance and a need to flatter their egos, so they naturally contemplate occupational choices to meet these outsized emotional needs.

"While alcoholism occurs in every occupation, positions that inflate the ego attract early-stage alcoholics," said Aaron. "Out of respect for the professions, we tend to think that doctors, lawyers, pilots, politicians, entertainers, and law enforcement personnel are less likely to become alcoholics. But just the opposite is true. Such careers fulfill the need of the alcoholic to stand out, be special and important, and they are chosen long before any excessive drinking begins."

"They do the right kind of things," said Jason, "for the wrong kinds of reasons."

"As alcoholism progresses to the middle stage, many alcoholics change jobs to keep work from interfering with their drinking,"

*

*Alcoholics don't
need chaos
in their lives;
they demand it.*

*

Aaron continued. "They move into consulting, outside sales, or buy a franchise so they can be their own boss. Workers with manual skills move to easier, less taxing jobs like painting, hanging wallpaper, or landscaping."

"Okay," said Jason, "I have a problem here. Say you have two high achieving executives. Which one is the alcoholic?"

"Maybe neither, maybe both," Aaron replied quickly. "But if you want to compare and contrast a high-achieving alcoholic with a high achiever, the whole case usually boils down to the difference between two words: one leader talks about people who work *for* him, while the other talks about people who work *with* him. One leader takes all the credit for any accomplishments, and the other shares the success as a team effort. The alcoholic has a huge sense of self-importance. He acts as though everyone should feel fortunate to work for him."

"And the other guy?" asks Jason, anticipating the bullet.

"The other has genuine humility. Humility is the key difference," said Aaron. "The leadership qualities needed and ultimately successful are a healthy sense of personal humility combined with a strong will. That's according to the popular business author, Jim Collins.[14]

"The alcoholic leader, by contrast, must constantly inflate his ego because he suffers from a bloated sense of self-importance. He has a superior attitude that requires and expects the admiration and even the reverence of others.

"The genuinely humble leader appreciates his talents and skills as gifts, not personal achievements. One can be a great person and at the same time practice humility. The truly humble person isn't compelled to avoid asking for help, because for him it isn't demeaning to do so. He knows that he needs other people.

"The person with the inflated ego, a bloated self-image, never seems satisfied," Aaron continued. "His false sense of superiority makes him feel he always deserves more. He feels personally attacked when coworkers directly disagree with him—or even when things just go wrong. He thinks, 'How dare this happen to me?'

"For example, I once criticized a client's decision in front of a few employees. He blew up like an H-bomb. He just went nuts. I had never seen such a thing before. Later, in private, he told me I shouldn't talk to him that way because—get this—'I am me.'"

"You're kidding!" exclaimed an astonished Jason. "His position was *I am me*?"

"He had no other way to excuse his behavior," said Aaron. "Of course, I had no idea his ego was that fragile. I apologized for creating a scene, though he never did. People unable to say, simply, 'I apologize' have quite the inflated ego."

"The subject of humility is a big one," said Jason. "I read a great deal about humility in a religion class I took, but I need to be better at seeing it in business."

"I just described two type of leaders. Think about this, Jason: if you were going to enter into a business relationship with one of these executives, who would you choose, all things being equal?"

"Okay, point made," Jason nodded. "Success is good, but certainly not the only good. I would definitely want my partner to have a good sense of humility if I were going into a business deal that depended on him."

"The effect of alcoholism is far greater than just a hangover, "Aaron said. "Being flexible enough to adjust and change calls for some humility. There's no change without humility, and no progress

*

*Humility doesn't mean
thinking any less of yourself;
it means thinking of yourself less.*

*

without change. Why should the alcoholic, with his superior attitude, change anything? Keep this in mind. A person who is at home in reality, as they say, isn't driven to be superior, to be right all the time, or to be on top of everyone and everything. If he needs help, he has no difficulty asking for it."

On that note, Aaron finished his coffee and he and Jason wrapped it up for the day. Aaron asked Jason to think about the ways alcoholics might wield power over other people in an office and to come up with a list of examples for their morning meeting. As for Jason, he was ready for a break after a day's work, and another briefing on alcoholism with his mentor.

Aaron and Jason got off to a later start than usual the next morning, and they arrived at the Waffle House just after the breakfast traffic had peaked. They sat in a corner booth and enjoyed a relaxed meal.

"We covered a great deal yesterday," said Jason.

"Let's pick up where we left off," said Aaron. "We were talking about the alcoholic ego—the 'Supreme-Being complex.' This phenomenon has many other clues, such as positioning oneself to wield power over others.

"This kind of power is a significant ego-inflating behavior trait," he continued as the waitress refreshed his cup of coffee. "Aware of it or not, early-stage alcoholics gravitate toward jobs in which they can rule over other people. Examples vary based on the culture. On the respectable side of economic status, we find doctors, lawyers, politicians, teachers, law enforcement agents, prison guards, and, in general, being the 'boss.' At the lower end of the scale are roles such as gang leader, drug dealer, bookie, and being the 'player' that everybody looks up to."

"I thought of a few ways alcoholics can inflate their egos by wielding power over others on the job," said Jason.

"Great!" said Aaron. "Let's hear them."

"What about firing people?" said Jason. "You know—intimidation, belittling others."

"Very good," replied Aaron. "Be quick to determine whether a firing is an actual business necessity or just a display of power that pumps up the boss's ego. In the latter case, he'll typically beat his chest and let people know, sometimes in subtle ways, that he had to exercise his power for the good of the company."

"Intimidation is a good way to inflate one's ego," said Jason. "It's a tactic used by people who have to be right all the time—those who have to win every argument and have the last word."

"That's a good one too," said Aaron. "Yelling, huffing and puffing, or throwing things all indicate a need to win at any and all costs."

"There's also the person that everyone tiptoes around, as if they were on thin ice whenever he's around," said Jason. "The guy who puts everyone on the defensive."

"Yep, that's another intimidation tactic," Aaron nodded. "That guy creates a tense, explosive atmosphere around himself, as if he'll blow like Mount St. Helens at any minute. He keeps people on their guard, so they're always checking, waiting for just the right moment before they even ask him a question. Behind his back, the staff asks each other how Captain Bligh is doing—'Is a tsunami predicted for today?' Remarks like that.

"Of course," Aaron went on, "there's always the guy who continually knocks everybody else, belittling them to elevate himself by comparison. That's classic ego-inflating behavior. It can vary from subtle disparagement to petty insults and blatant put-downs."

"Let's carry that tendency a step further," said Jason. "What about racism?"

"Sure," Aaron nodded. "Claiming superiority to another race is ego inflation on a grand scale. Such large targets of hate reinforce the alcoholic's ego-inflated, deluded sense of superiority and importance. He builds himself up by tearing down whole groups of people, by race, nationality, ethnicity, gender, or sexual orientation."

"That behavior touches on many things besides alcoholism in the workplace," said Jason, "but it applies anyway. I don't see any of these behaviors as proof-positive of alcoholism. But the presence of any one of them, or, especially, a combination of them, in a person's behavioral repertoire is a definite warning sign of possible alcoholism."

"Exactly," said Aaron. "Awareness and alertness are the keys. We look for alcoholism because it's so common, and a common source of serious business problems at every stage of its progression."

"The disease seems to focus on power," Jason said.

"Yes," said Aaron, "and while we're speaking of abusing power over others, another big issue comes to mind. All consultants probably encounter it, but they don't recognize it for what it is. It's the tendency of some people to refuse responsibility for anything that goes wrong, and, instead, always blaming other people for the problems and snafus that occur. That sort of thing is not really a hallmark of humility or good leadership."

"How does it work, exactly?" said Jason.

"The guy has an attitude of superiority—he's too competent and skilled to have made the mistake in question—which is any mistake at all," said Aaron. "He always blames someone else and pumps up his own ego by correcting the 'incompetents.' He can't ever find strength in the admission of a simple mistake. You'll never hear him say 'I was wrong.'"

"That reminds me of your point yesterday about the humility of real leaders versus the egotism of alcoholic leaders," said Jason. "The inability to admit a mistake shows a profound lack of humility."

"You're getting the picture," said Aaron, sipping his coffee and then going on. "A variation on laying the blame on others is the habit of blowing problems out of all proportion and then rushing in to save the day, play the great man on the white horse, the only one who can set things right. How's that for wielding power? His coworkers may watch in disbelief as Our Hero takes an ordinary difficulty and blows it up into Mount Everest, then saves the day. His whole attitude says:

'Look at what I have to do. I'm always pulling you guys out of the fire.' It's all 'me, me, me.'"

Aaron detailed other ways in which budding alcoholics play blame games and evade responsibility for errors on the job. All these behaviors indicate low self-esteem, a common characteristic among alcoholics. Someone who has a balanced view of himself can easily accept that he has made a mistake. Recognizing errors and correcting them indicate maturity and humility. But a person with low self esteem has to compensate for his low self-regard by cultivating an attitude of superiority and infallibility.

"Never defend a mistake!" Said Aaron. "It doesn't work. The truth always comes out, sooner or later. The single defect of character that probably causes more misery than any other is this inability to say, 'I was wrong. I apologize."

Jason said, "What about the know-it-all who talks down to everyone and seems to have all the answers? Doesn't that signal an inflated sense of self-importance, a problem with genuine self-esteem?"

"Sure it does," said Aaron. "The most noticeable difference between someone with real knowledge imparting help or teaching something and the windbag who just pontificates is the latter's arrogant, cocky manner. Think about the people who like to use high-sounding language, insider's lingo, and other jargon, instead of plain English. Those word choices convey subtly that the speaker possesses rare knowledge, privileged information to which 'mere human beings' don't have access."

"I know a few MBAs like that," Jason smiled.

*

My opinions may have changed, but not the fact that I am right.

*

"T hose are just a few examples," said Aaron. "Have you thought of any more ways alcoholics can abuse their power over others?"

After a moment, Jason said, "What about the guy who's always calling meetings so he can sit at the head of a long table and have everyone respond to his questions, directions, and—well, his whims?"

"Perfect," Aaron smiled. "Especially when there's no real need for the meeting, which is usually apparent once the hour is wasted. He just likes to hear himself talk, to show that he's in charge, to command the floor and call on people."

"And have the last word," said Jason.

"Of course," Aaron said. "These types create a costly business expense by taking people away from the real work that makes sales and actually moves the company forward. Holding meetings may be a way to simply wield control and inflate one's own ego."

Aaron told Jason about a client whose sales manager had a mandatory meeting at 4:00 every Friday. "He pulled sales reps back to the office from appointments all over the city, so he could listen to them discuss their week. This was followed by a session in which he would demean or insult selected employees in front of the others."

"That's really awful," said Jason.

Aaron nodded. "Of course, once the meeting ended, all the reps were welcome to join the boss at the local watering hole for a Friday afternoon drink. In other words, they had to legitimize his drinking."

"Did the management ever catch on?"

"Sure, after enough complaints," said Aaron. "He also exhibited a few other obnoxious behaviors, and eventually they promoted him out of sales manager and transferred him to another office.

"Speaking of meetings, there's another common office tool that alcoholics can use to the advantage of their disease," Aaron said. "Can you guess what it is?"

Jason thought hard for a moment, then his face brightened a little and he said, "How about the telephone?"

"Precisely," Aaron smiled at his protégé. "The phone can work the same way meetings do—as another power trip. The egotist calls all the time, or at all times of day. And now that we have cell phones, we're expected to be available at any time, so the guy can dominate others with useless questions during off-hours. Calls like that let us know that the wonder boy is always on the job, and he gets a thrill by making everybody else jump to his schedule and disrupt their own. He uses the phone to control others.

"This sort of 'telephonitis' is just another way to dominate others and abuse power," Aaron continued. "Such a person can barely drive his car without making a call on his cell phone. And of course, don't forget that the ultimate telephone ego-inflating power trip: the abrupt hang up."

"That's quite a list," said Jason. "Do you have any others?"

"I can think of two that occur outside the office," said Aaron. "Sexual exploitation and road rage."

"What could be more ego-inflating and controlling than perpetually sleeping around?" Aaron asked. "The king of the one-night stand, the 'ladies man,' always lets everyone know about his latest conquest, typically starting the conversation by saying, 'Don't tell anyone.'" Aaron laughed. "Some reports say that alcoholism is a factor in half of all divorces. Surely adultery, which is common among alcoholics, is a big factor here. Of course, the ladies man always has a good—make that *rational*—reason why the rules of human sexual behavior don't apply to him."

"And road rage?" said Jason.

"That's another example that may seem like a stretch, but which fits in many cases," said Aaron. "A driver with serious road rage acts as if his needs are more important than those of others, and that the rules don't apply to him. Road rage may be symptomatic of alcoholism. Of course, I'm not talking about the common frustration everyone experiences in traffic. The guy with the problem has a rapid, raging, angry response to other drivers."

"You keep mentioning the idea of the alcoholic's exemption from the rules everyone else lives by," Jason said. "I take it that's a common character trait."

"That attitude usually comes paired with a feeling of invincibility," said Aaron. "What can be more ego inflating than the belief that rules are for other people, not you? Imagine how dangerous such thinking can be in a person with control over money or someone in a position to place a company in legal jeopardy."

"That applies from the top jobs all the way down to entry-level positions," Jason said.

"Definitely," Aaron nodded. "Alcoholics see themselves as unique—special people.

"Another trait of early-stage alcoholism is lying," said Aaron. "In fact, you could say that lying encompasses all the other traits."

Jason nodded. "Lying definitely jeopardizes any business venture," he said. "It creates confusion, impairs understanding, and demoralizes employees."

"Lying is another ego-inflating behavior," Aaron continued. "In part, the alcoholic lies just to prove to himself that he can get away with it. By lying—even when he has no reason to—he wields power over others secretly. He knows the truth, and knowledge is power, right? His co-workers and friends receive the altered facts and get shorted on the truly relevant information. The early-stage alcoholic employee will also use the power of this kind of falsehood to make false accusations."

"I've been on the receiving end of conversations that start with 'Don't tell this to anyone' and 'Now, if you repeat this, I'll deny it,'" said Jason. "That sort of talk has destroyed a lot of reputations -- cost people their jobs and triggered lawsuits."

"True enough," said Aaron, "and sometimes the lie isn't outright. It's simply an inflation of random circumstantial evidence or withholding relevant information.

"But the really funny thing is that the person lying never thinks he'll be found out, and sooner or later, he always is."

"Sure!" said Jason. "The alcoholic, in particular, thinks he is special—clever and undetectable. The ordinary rules of honesty just don't apply to him."

"Sometimes, he doesn't actually lie. He really doesn't know the truth because he was in an alcoholic blackout," said Aaron. "He can't admit to this temporary amnesia, of course, so he makes up something. And what he can recall, he remembers in a self-favoring light."

"So lying can be another kind of rationalizing," said Jason.

"You're right," Aaron replied. "It's more of alcoholism's 'rational lies.'"

"I once had a client who bragged that he hadn't had a driver's license for over a year," said Aaron.

"Rather a strange achievement," said Jason.

"I thought so, too. But it was a matter of ego inflation. Taking legal liberties and bending the law should be a red flag in the office, or anywhere else. The behavior can seem minor, like parking in a fire zone when a legal spot is only yards away. But significant infractions include matters of taxes, payroll, and expenses fraud."

"I know a guy who always pushes things to the limit of the law," said Jason. "I can see that as an ego trip."

"It's not that he's a criminal, or consciously trying to break the law," said Aaron. "In the alcoholic's mind, he can't do any wrong. Not really. It's the rules that are wrong. He has a 'good' reason, a 'rational' reason for his acts. It's hard to think of a worse business decision than not paying employee withholdings into the Payroll Tax Trust Fund; but an alcoholic could do it—for the good of the employees and the company's growth."

"He could put the company out of business," said Jason, "or go broke paying heavy penalties, not to mention the risk of jail time."

"All true," said Aaron. "But he'll think of it as 'doing good,' rather than intentionally violating the law and hurting everyone. Such people pose serious dangers to the employees, the investors, the banks, and to themselves."

"And they all appear to be perfectly rational human beings."

"The problem hides in plain sight, remember?" Aaron said. "Another common legal liberty in small businesses is check-kiting—issuing a check without sufficient funds in the hope or expectation that a deposit will come in and cover the amount. You'll hear the guy say, 'They told me the check was sent via FedEx, and I trusted them!'"

"So he can blame someone else when his check is returned NSF," Jason said.

"Of course, right up there with the other risky behaviors of alcoholics is driving under the influence," said Aaron.

"I don't see how getting one DUI or DWI proves alcoholism," replied Jason.

"No, one DUI doesn't prove alcoholism, although it sure is a warning," Aaron said. "But continuing to drink and drive after suffering the consequences of a DUI, and getting pulled again for a second DUI, strongly suggests alcoholism."

"A friend of mine who quit drinking says that being ticketed for DUI saved her life," Jason remarked. "She says it still scares her when she thinks of how many times she didn't get caught."

"If a person has two or more DUIs, assume a high likelihood of alcoholism," said Aaron. "In the early stages, the high tolerance of many alcoholics fools the police. This experience gives drunk drivers a false sense of security. Sometimes, a guy will even brag about how he gets away with it. The situation covers several traits: the attitude that 'the rules don't apply to me' and the idea that he is a superior person, that he is too smart and too careful to get caught."

"I have a friend from B-school who seems to get away with driving drunk," said Jason. "Once when he got pulled over, he made sure the policeman saw his expired Marine ID when he showed his driver's license. The cop told him to drive carefully and thanked him for his service."

"Uniforms enabling uniforms," said Aaron.

"Virtually every alcoholic has financial problems," Aaron continued. "He is leveraged to the max. Playing the big spender who can afford everything inflates his ego, while, in reality, he's always struggling to pay for his fancy car or his big house. His compulsive spending is a big ego inflator even while it drives him deeper and deeper into debt. The business owner or salesperson suffering from the distorted perception and impaired judgment of alcoholism tells himself that the big payoff is right around the corner. He's just advancing the money he knows is coming soon. But when the big payoff doesn't come—and it rarely does—he has to blame someone else."

Identifying the Early Stage
- Ego-Inflating Behaviors
  - Overachiever, must win at any cost
  - Stress junkie
  - Job choices and pursuits
- Wielding Power over Others
  - Firing people
  - Intimidation
  - Walking on thin ice
  - Belittles others
  - Racism and hatred of people
  - Blame game
  - Pontificates
  - Excessive meetings and conference calls
  - Telephonitis
  - Serial sexual exploitation
  - Road rage
- Sense of Invincibility, Risky Behaviors, Rules Don't Apply to Me
  - Lying
  - Legal liberties
  - DUI
  - Compulsive spender

That afternoon, Aaron and Jason met again at the Starbucks across from Coyle's.

"The key to recognizing alcoholism consists of spotting the clues early and then protecting yourself and your company," said Aaron. "Anyone entering into a key business relationship should proceed with caution if he suspects alcoholism."

"I see that, and I understand the dangers especially in light of the progressive nature of the disease," Jason replied. "I have to admit that I wouldn't see the clues to early-stage alcoholism if I weren't looking for them—things like a person's ego inflation, bloated self-importance, and sense of special exception that the ordinary rules don't apply to him. A sense of the behavioral symptoms gives us a new understanding of alcoholism."

"To be fair though," Aaron said, "we need to remember that 85-90 percent of drinkers can drink alcohol normally and safely. Let's not go on a prohibitionist witch hunt. I'm not anti-alcohol, just anti-alcoholic behaviors. The rule of thumb is not 'just say no' but 'just say no to alcoholic behaviors.'

"As the alcoholic progresses to the middle stage of the disease," Aaron continued, "his maladaptive behaviors grow more obvious, and the damage begins to be much more serious. It becomes quantifiable and measurable.

"Occupational choice may evolve," he explained. "As drinking becomes a priority in life in very subtle ways, the alcoholic gravitates to jobs that don't interfere with his drinking.

"We all know the joke that *consultant* is another word for *unemployed*," Aaron laughed ironically. "Many an alcoholic, approaching the middle stage, goes into sales, where he is not closely managed or observed, just accountable for satisfying a sales quota. He becomes skilled at scheduling calls around his hangovers and mental fogs while still achieving the sale. Should he become unemployable—possibly because others are beginning to catch on to his problems—his inflated ego and bloated sense of self-importance may encourage him to buy a franchise. The difficult creative work is done for him in a franchise, but he can still devote time to the legwork necessary to grow the business. After all, he knows he can run a business better than anyone else, and best of all, he can be his own boss, accountable to no one, and working around his hangovers and drinking."

"I know several people who are working below their education and skill level—working with their hands, doing light labor or sales," said Jason. "Maybe they're accommodating their drinking."

"Before I invest in helping someone start a franchise or new company, I look carefully for any signs of alcoholism," said Aaron. "It only gets worse, never better.

"In the middle stage, performance definitely starts to decline," said Aaron. "Quotas go unmet, goals unachieved, and promises not kept. Remember the strange quirk of alcoholism, the grand paradox, that early-stage alcoholics are usually high achievers who perform very well," said Aaron. "In the middle stage, the increasingly distorted perceptions and impaired judgment contribute to declining results and performance. The downward slide of the progression begins to be noticeable to others, although the cause—alcoholism—is still well hidden most of the time."

Jason said, "I suppose that bosses and coworkers start making excuses, maybe just to themselves, during the decline."

"I've heard things like 'the top dog's having an off-year,' and 'maybe he has problems at home,' and 'you can't win every year,'" said Aaron.

"Nobody wants to address the real issue of alcoholism," said Jason, "or else they don't recognize it."

"Right," said Aaron. "By this point, the alcoholic is more focused on a drink, although usually unconsciously. His work becomes more talk than reality. As they say in Texas, he becomes 'all hat, no cattle.'"

Aaron went on to say that the active alcoholic does not take responsibility for his decline. Since he remembers everything about himself in a favorable light, it is next to impossible for him to take such responsibility. He thinks, "I can't be at fault—look at my record," though his past high achievement in the early stage also resulted from the alcoholic drive to be better than everyone else in compensation for his low self-esteem. He shifts the blame for current failures onto others and lobbies his coworkers to agree with his warped judgment of who

*

*What's the difference between
a drunk and an alcoholic?*

*A drunk will steal your wallet.
An alcoholic will steal your wallet
and help you look for it.*

*

is really at fault. He does this even when no one else really cares. The alcoholic perpetually seeks the support of imagined allies for his own declining judgment. The other employees begin to realize what he is doing and pull away from their former friend. They develop personal and professional doubts and mistrust.

"Deteriorating judgment becomes increasingly common as alcoholism progresses in the middle state," explained Aaron.

"I remember what I read about the biology of alcoholism," said Jason, "how the perception centers in the neocortex of the brain become damaged."

"Right," said Aaron. "You're seeing how all the pieces ultimately fit together. With his perception increasingly distorted by the disease's progression and with his consumption of alcohol increasing as well, we begin to see his former good decision-making abilities diluted and impaired.

"At this point, we commonly notice another trait of advancing alcoholism: mental confusion," said Aaron. "The employee may appear to be in a fog, unable to fully follow a conversation or set of instructions. He is slowly becoming 'a mess,' with a shorter attention span and difficulties multitasking."

"I imagine people tend to accommodate them," said Jason, "to give them less to do and try not to overwhelm them."

"That's the beginning of financial loss for the company," Aaron nodded. "You can add to that increasing errors, sloppy mistakes, lost work and paper, and an overall work slowdown on the alcoholic's part."

Aaron explained the issue in more clinical terms as well. The alcoholic's body expects, needs, and craves alcohol to maintain a base blood alcohol content (BAC). The lowering of BAC can lead to mental confusion. Confusion also occurs when the BAC is too *high*. By a strange quirk of alcoholism, the middle-stage alcoholic seems to exhibit his sharpest mental clarity after only a few drinks—just enough to satisfy the alcohol needs of his body and his brain chemistry.

"I know of a few people who seem brightest and most together during happy hour," Jason said.

"Sure," Aaron nodded. "They're just getting themselves together and are on their game, while their coworkers are tired from the day and are checking out the scene around the bar."

Aaron continued: "Increasing tardiness, or absence on a certain day after a night of drink specials—these are major red flags of middle-stage alcoholism."

Jason replied: "Hungover alcoholics certainly don't feel very well, though they try to hide it. They attempt to cover the dismal condition with some excuse or 'rational lie,' like 'it must have been something I ate.'"

"Just plain going missing, or having unexplained absences, are sure signs of an increasing alcohol problem," said Aaron.

"In the office," he continued, "increasing personality conflicts develop around the alcoholic. He becomes harder and harder to work with. He's irritable, easily upset, argumentative, and quick to retaliate with reactionary, even harsh comments. Such behavior can result from alcohol withdrawals or hangover."

"That's interesting," said Jason, "because he can honestly say that he hasn't had a drink in several days, but not drinking is actually what's causing his foul mood."

"Exactly," said Aaron. "He's in a perpetual ill humor because he's constantly withdrawing from alcohol, causing a drop in dopamine, or he's suffering from an ongoing mild hangover that he's 'learned to live with.' Old friends and office allies aren't such pals anymore. His tendency to blame others for his difficulties turns people away and they begin to avoid him. Friends at work can only roll their eyes. They begin to treat the alcoholic as increasingly irrelevant. When coworkers complain, they're told things like 'that's just how he is,' which unintentionally lowers the standard for his declining behavior. Such excuses actually enable alcoholic behavior.

"Another telltale sign of likely alcoholism is increasing trouble at home, including divorce," Aaron said. "Several studies estimate that 50-70 percent of all divorces involve alcoholism.[15] By that, the researchers really mean the behaviors arising from alcoholism. These estimates may be high, but we should be especially cautious toward people with multiple divorces in their pasts."

"People with special sets of rules for their conduct, who regularly have to inflate their egos, can be awfully difficult to live with," said Jason.

"When you step back and look at the various behaviors associated with alcoholism, it's no surprise relationships deteriorate," Aaron noted. "And we haven't even talked about what some studies suggest as a leading cause of divorce: Money issues.

"Increasing financial difficulty is a consistent red flag that identifies progressing alcoholism," said Aaron. "Level of income doesn't seem to matter. Almost all middle- and late-stage alcoholics have increasing financial problems. I have several very wealthy alcoholic clients with financial problems who now relate to their money differently than they did earlier in the disease. They each make a solid six-figure income, but they are broke. A person with financial difficulties, regardless of his position in a company, is extremely dangerous. If he has access to company funds, added precautions or removal from access to funds becomes immediately necessary."

"I've know a few rich people who complain about their finances and tax returns," Jason commented with a smile. "I always laugh to myself, and think they are lucky to have such problems."

*

*Alcohol gave me
wings to fly,
but then it took
away the sky.*

*

"Watch out for employees who borrow money, ask for a paycheck advance, or have trouble fronting minor business expense money before reimbursement," Aaron cautioned. "Alcoholism should be suspected. Also, think how destructive an alcoholic executive or owner is who can legally give himself cash advances."

Jason nodded. "Living beyond your means is a definite sign of ego inflation, distorted perception, and bad judgment."

"Of course, tough financial situations develop in the real world," Aaron said. "A spouse gets laid off; there is an unexpected expense, a health issue or a major car repair. But alcoholism should always be considered.

"Here is how the finances evolve as alcoholism progresses," he went on. "The early-stage alcoholic, with his inflated view of himself, increases his easy debt, usually with credit cards. He knows that, since he is so talented and productive, a big check, or a new deal or job, is just waiting around the corner and will enable him to pay off his debt. Oops! The disease progresses, the big check or new job doesn't come through, and credit cards and other sources of funds, like borrowing from relatives, get maxed out and cut off. His financial difficulties increase, cell phones and utilities are cut off, and he's juggling his bill payments. At work, he can't front even small business expenses and has to ask for expense advances. The crisis level rises as his shortsighted, panicked judgment increases. There's no telling what he may do, goaded on by ever-greater rationalizations."

"You would want to watch expense reports and overtime," said Jason. "Also, if the guy is in sales, he may exaggerate claims in order to sell a product, and the customer will catch on eventually. Such an unhappy customer could really hurt a business."

"It can happen in any number of ways," said Aaron. "That's why it's important to identify alcoholism as early as possible and implement effective safeguards."

"There's also a very funny but very real warning sign," said Aaron: "the person has 'rules' for his drinking. He may even advertise his rules to others. He makes sure everyone knows he doesn't drink on weeknights; or he only has two on work nights; he just drinks beer or wine during the week, but enjoys his Jack Daniels on weekends; he only drinks at home; he never drinks alone; he never mixes beer with liquor; or he only drinks with a meal; and on and on, *ad infinitum*. Think about such rules: normal drinkers don't have them. They don't need them. They drink alcohol in a normal, healthy fashion. Only alcoholics need rules for drinking. The funny thing is that by announcing their rules they're really announcing their preoccupation with alcohol, which is a major sign of alcoholism.

"The advanced drinker thinks he knows all the tricks so that no one notices," Aaron smiled grimly. "His breath smells like candy or chewing gum or a breath spray. He plans ahead; with cover-ups for alcohol always close at hand—the breath spray or mints, candy in the car—always ready to cover up a chance that someone might notice he has been drinking.

"He falls prey to the law of unintended consequences: Detection increases the more he tries to avoid detection. It's all even more obvious once your antenna is up, on the alert for drinking problems."

"And let's not forget what a serious disease alcoholism is," Aaron cautioned. "As it progresses, in addition to increasing bad behaviors, there are growing mental and physical health problems.

"Depression is common among all alcoholics," he went on. "The symptoms of middle-stage alcoholism mimic symptoms of other mental health issues. Ultimately, if the alcoholism isn't arrested, mental issues such as depression become permanent or become masked by a wide range of antidepressants. Depression affects everyone at some time in his life, but it seems to be a part of almost every alcoholic's existence. Certainly some people need help and treatment for depression in addition to alcoholism."

"It's interesting," said Jason, "that the stigma of depression is fading—people are more willing to talk about it and seek help. But it seems that the stigma surrounding alcoholism—that it's a weakness or a result of bad character—keeps many from asking for help or even being open to the idea of it."

"Public education has helped erase the stigma of depression," Aaron noted, "and hopefully we'll start seeing more of the same concerning alcoholism.

"Alcoholism incurs its cost to business in many ways," Aaron said. "One way is accidents, which increase insurance and worker's compensation costs. Accidents, scrapes, cuts, and bruises don't just happen. If you notice frequent 'battle scars' on employees, it's fair to suspect alcoholism. Such injuries may be the result of drunkenness. If the employee's explanation for his wounds is extremely long or detailed, that's a red flag for a hidden alcohol impairment. Normal drinkers just trip on a curb and fall, but the alcoholic always has an elaborate story to tell, putting himself in the favorable light of hapless victimhood.

"Illnesses that are unusual for a person's age also flag alcoholism," said Aaron. "Alcoholism can be associated with a wide range of health issues, such as gastrointestinal, cardiac, and skin problems. The business suffers from absences, poor performance, and increasing insurance costs related to alcoholism. It can get even worse in this litigious world if the alcoholic tries to blame the company for his illness.

"Another person to watch for," Aaron continued, "is the guy who moves to a new city without any job or plans. Alcoholics, without necessarily being aware of it, often resort to such 'geographic cures' in attempts to relieve their increasing distress."

*

*Alcoholics can be
found at the airport
waiting for their
ships to come in.*

*

"What if someone wonders whether he is an alcoholic?" asked Jason.

"It may sound simplistic," Aaron said with a gentle smile, "but if someone wonders whether he has alcoholism, he probably does. Normal drinkers don't wonder because they have no reason to."

"By the time a person has entered the final stage of alcoholism, it's unlikely he is still employed," said Aaron. "His constant confusion, continual health problems, and the simple difficulty of being around him make him fundamentally unemployable."

"What if he's the boss?" Jason asked.

"Employees have to look out for themselves," said Aaron. "If the company is headed down, they may want to look for other jobs. The more entrepreneurial types may consider starting a competing company or even buying their company from the late-stage alcoholic boss. Hopefully, they'll have made some efforts to encourage their boss to get help, even if they have to talk to his family."

Characteristics of Middle Stage

- Job downgrading
- Underachiever, poor performance
- Commitments not kept
- Poor judgment
- Mental confusion
- Tardy and absent
- Increasing personality conflicts
- Divorce or trouble at home
- Increasing financial problems
- Has rules for drinking
- Hides odor
- Depression
- Accidents
- Unusual illnesses for age
- Geographic changes
- Wonders if he or she is an alcoholic

*

*If you think you
may have a
drinking problem,
you just might.*

*

PART 3:

THERE IS NO GOOD TIME
TO ACT — EXCEPT NOW

The next morning, Jason met Aaron at the Waffle House for another breakfast. He had done some reading the night before, and asked Aaron about the roles, responses, and responsibilities of the various people around the alcoholic—his coworkers, employers, friends, and family.

Aaron had heard the question before. "Just as alcoholics grow into masters of denial and rationalization, the people around them generally develop an attitude that we call 'learned helplessness,'" he said. "They adapt to and accommodate the difficult situations arising from the alcoholic's drinking. They are as trapped in the alcoholic cycle as the alcoholic is. 'Learned helplessness' results from a wearing-down process involving stress, erratic behavior—theirs as well as the alcoholic's—and having a sense of no control or influence in their own lives—a feeling of powerlessness and unmanageability. We learn to tolerate bad behavior and accept that the nuisance can't be avoided. We do this when we lower the behavioral bar for the alcoholic.

A business suffering from such learned helplessness may find itself in a situation in which the limitations of an employee, or a group of employees, control the entire company," Aaron continued. "The executives, managers, and coworkers accept those limitations and adapt to them, instead of demanding compliance with company standards. They ought to be leading, training, and communicating. Instead, they adopt the limitations of the dysfunctional.

"One of my clients has a group of workers in the field who won't enter data correctly in their online order flow system," Aaron said. "Management has learned to accommodate the employees—to work around them. In other words, they learned to be helpless. They allow the tail to wag the dog.

*

*If a person has a thousand
problems, and one of the
problems is alcoholism,
then he has only one problem.*

*

"Learned helplessness is an unconscious way of enabling the alcoholic and other dysfunctional behaviors. It amounts to management's willful surrender," Aaron said.

"When we started a few weeks ago, I was curious about why you wanted me to learn about alcoholism," said Jason. "Now I see it: It doesn't take many alcoholics in a business to create substantial problems. If they're in key positions, that's double trouble. Alcoholics decline while everyone else tries to grow a business and make money."

"From what you've learned so far," Aaron asked, "what stands out the most?"

"First, I have to remember that most people who drink don't have a problem and that there's nothing wrong with drinking alcohol per se," Jason replied. "The other factor is the progressive nature of alcoholism as a disease. I used to think in black and white: alcoholic or not alcoholic. I didn't consider that an alcoholic's behavior evolves through stages as his disease progresses."

"That's why people in business need to recognize the symptoms of alcoholism at the earliest possible stage and protect their interests first," Aaron noted quickly. "Then they need to decide the best course of action to take in dealing with the suspected alcoholic.

"Denial of our awareness of actual circumstances occurs all the time, whether a person has alcoholism or not," said Aaron. "At times, we all wish that ignoring a problem will make it disappear, and sometimes it does! But alcoholism doesn't just go away. All sorts of things get worse. Odds are overwhelming that the alcoholic will continue to drink until an accumulation of crises forces him to experience and face the consequences of his actions."

"All too often, people with a full awareness of the disease and its progressive nature know an alcoholic who is headed for a train wreck, and they still sit back and do nothing," Aaron noted. "They resign themselves to being the co-victims of the person's alcoholism. In reality, the knowledgeable employer is in the strongest position to act by enforcing real consequences for the alcoholic's behavior, both the drinking and its effects. The informed employer can do a great

*

*He went from being
a novelty to being a train
wreck and bypassed
the interesting stage.*

*

deal early on to lead the drinker to a sober life for him and for the business.

"I have lost a great many friends to alcoholism," Aaron paused to reflect. "That's very frustrating because alcoholism is treatable. We can avoid the damage if we take early action. We must start somewhere, and education is a good start. The alcoholic may resist and evade it, but the seed of recovery can be planted. Deep down, an awareness may emerge. In most cases, though, a heavier hammer needs to be used: The threat of job loss is one of the strongest leverage points that can influence an alcoholic."

"And the loss of his driver's license," Jason laughed.

"That's the point," said Aaron. "We must find the leverage point with the greatest impact, and since we work with employers, the alcoholic's job and income form a good, solid beginning. The job lever—the risk of losing his job because of alcoholism—can have a crucial effect on the alcoholic, leading him to stop drinking, hopefully before he gets a DUI or worse," Aaron said.

"But don't some people avoid action because they think that nothing will work until the alcoholic 'hits bottom'?" Jason asked.

"Some people sincerely believe that and watch the train wreck happen," Aaron shook his head sadly. "But some use that attitude to avoid their personal discomfort at confronting a friend or coworker about his drinking and run the risk of a scene, or of losing a friend.

"That's why I say that alcoholics don't hit bottom alone," Aaron continued. "The alcoholic takes captives along the way, sharing his misery with the friends and others who can't or won't confront him about his obvious problem. That way, he bounces off a bottom for years. And he has more than scrapes and bruises to show for it: He is enabled by 'friends,' who don't appreciate the damage to which they are accomplices. His enabling friends tell him not to worry, that all his problems will work out, or that he's just having a run of bad luck. In the case of the truly codependent relationship, the erstwhile friend enables the alcoholic by sticking by him no matter what happens, basking in the glow of the roles of Rescuer and Self-Sacrificing Friend."

"Aaron, I hear the phrase 'hitting bottom' used around alcoholism and addiction," said Jason. "What exactly is a *bottom* when talking about alcoholism?"

"The bottom of alcoholism occurs when a combination of crises finally becomes intolerable to the individual alcoholic," Aaron said. "The impossible happens: Betty Ford finds out that her whole family knows about her drinking, which she thought was a well-kept secret she had under control. One guy I knew hit his bottom trying to go to work one morning, simply because he couldn't get his car key in the ignition. Others lose their job, home, family—they lose it all. Whatever form it takes, the pain of the effects of drinking finally outweighs the pleasure of the drink itself. The alcoholic's over-sized ego finally screams for help."

Aaron retrieved some copies from his briefcase and passed them across the table to Jason. "Alcoholism expert Abraham J. Twerski, M.D., looks at hitting bottom from an interesting angle," he said. "Basically he says the same thing I do, but he frames a bottom in a way that better illustrates what happens."

The Law of Human Gravity

A law of human behavior that appears as inviolable as the law of gravity might well be called the "law of human gravity": A person will gravitate from a condition that appears to be one of greater distress to a condition that appears to be one of lesser distress, and never in the reverse direction. According to this law, it is impossible for a person to choose greater distress. Any attempt to reverse the direction of the choice will be as futile as trying to make water flow uphill.

Alcohol and other mind-altering chemicals provide some measure of relief from discomfort, whether this is relief from anxiety, depression, loneliness, self-consciousness, or just the compulsive urge. Abstinence, at least initially, causes distress, sometimes psychological discomfort, and often severe physical discomfort.

If we try to get addicted people to stop alcohol or other chemical use, we are essentially asking them to choose a greater distress. But it is beyond human capacity to choose a greater distress. From this analysis it might appear that we should stop all efforts at treatment! Treatment can't work! But we know for a fact that treatment does work and that people do achieve sobriety. How does this happen?

Achieving Sobriety through Changes in Perception

While the law of human gravity is inviolable, and the direction can never change, it is possible for people to change their perceptions. People can learn to see chemical use as the greater distress and abstinence as the lesser distress.

Active addition:
Greater Distress: abstinence →Less Distress: use of chemicals

Recovery:
Greater Distress: use of chemicals →Less Distress: abstinence

How does this change of perception come about? All mind-altering chemicals sooner or later cause some kind of discomfort: the loss of respect from family and friends, the threat of losing a job, poor school performance, severe gastrointestinal symptoms, hangovers, hallucinations, falls and bruises, convulsive seizures, the distress of poor memory, the threat of imprisonment, or the terror of delusions.

When any of these, alone or in combination, reach the critical point— where the misery equals or exceeds whatever relief the chemical provides— then the person's perception of what is a greater or less distress changes.

This, then, is what happens when rock bottom occurs. Rock bottom is nothing more than a change of perception, where abstinence is seen as a lesser distress than use of chemicals. If at any time after abstinence is achieved, even many years later, abstinence becomes the greater distress, relapse will occur.

The natural course of addiction is such that rock bottom will come if no one interferes. But people in the addict's life, with every good intention, may remove some of the distresses that the chemical produces. For example, a coworker may cover for a colleague who is hung over. This prevents a change in perception of greater and lesser distress and permits the active addiction to continue. This is why people who remove the distressful consequences of chemical use are referred to as enablers.

Remember, allowing the natural unpleasant consequences to occur is not the same as punishing the user. Punishing is inflicting pain from the outside. If, for example, a drinker sees marriage as the source of distress, he or she will separate rather than quit drinking. Only when the alcoholic discovers that the drinking is causing the misery will sobriety become a solution.

Addicts' perceptions also change when they see the rewards of abstinence. When the rewards of abstinence begin to exceed the rewards of mind-altering chemicals, addicts can change their perceptions of which is the greater or lesser distress.[16]

"I like that," said Jason, "It pretty much says the same thing from a more analytical perspective. Thanks."

"Our challenge is: since alcoholics do have to hit bottom, how can we raise the bottom?" Aaron continued. "Rock bottom, the end of the road, is the classic image that persists: the skid row bum wandering into the Salvation Army meeting, that sort of thing. What if, instead, we think of the 'bottom' *as the turning point* at which the alcoholic's perceptions change? Looking at it that way, the goal of employers and friends becomes to raise the bottom, to avoid the despair of rock bottom."

"Okay, but now for the obvious question: How *do* we raise the bottom?" Jason asked.

"Two words," Aaron said: **"Stop enabling."**

"Okay," Jason nodded, "but I'm sure that's easier said than done."

"Of course," said Aaron. "We're much more comfortable pretending there's no pink elephant in the office. Unfortunately, we end up with a lot of pink elephant poop, which is real."

Jason laughed.

Aaron, smiling back, went on: "Most people don't suspect alcoholism in the early stages, but by the middle stages, they begin to realize that something isn't right. As the disease progresses and the alcoholic spirals downward, everyone around him is affected. Some are hurt more than others. Some realize what is happening, while most deny it."

"I see that," said Jason. "When we apologize or make excuses for the drinker, or brush off his screw-ups, we unconsciously enable him by preventing the natural *and necessary* consequences of his behavior from occurring."

"Exactly," said Aaron: "we become part of the problem. But if we let the chips fall where they may, we raise the bottom a little. *Any* relief from consequences enables the disease, and the alcoholic's continued drinking. People need to understand the disease—how it progresses, and how it affects the alcoholic's behavior—in order to *disenable* the alcoholic, to stop automatically and unconsciously enabling him."

"That kind of help doesn't feel like help to the alcoholic, though, does it?" Jason said.

"Well, a clearer understanding of what *help* actually is will clarify what we need to do. One kind of 'help'—the evasion of the natural consequences—keeps the alcoholic stuck in his disease, while the other 'help' offers him the possibility of recovery. One help 'enables' and nurtures the disease. The other 'help'—the genuine kind that we *should* care about—intervenes and interrupts the cycle of the disease so the alcoholic can get well."

"But it's much easier to enable, and definitely more comfortable," said Jason.

"It may be comfortable in the short-term, but the damage and cost will adversely affect everyone around the alcoholic sooner or later," said Aaron.

"As people learn more about alcoholism and its progressive nature and characteristics, they can more effectively identify potential alcoholics and protect their professional and personal interests. They can use whatever leverage they have to guide the alcoholic to help," said Aaron.

"A guy's job and his financial security can definitely get his attention," Jason nodded.

"Circumstances vary," said Aaron, "but the alcoholic must be confronted with the truth of his situation and condition. His attention, at least initially, will most likely be gained through the threat of painful, negative consequences."

"Won't the alcoholic resist?" said Jason. "Might he take the offensive and try to stop any efforts to interfere with his 'private life'?"

"Of course, and he'll have some 'rational' response," said Aaron. "That's precisely why the alcoholic needs to experience the negative consequences of his bad behavior. These consequences open his eyes to the truth of his condition. So, *enabling the consequences,* rather than the alcoholic, is the single best way to attack alcoholism. As I said, don't be afraid to let the chips fall where they may."

Then Aaron qualified his approach: "Of course, we have to remember that we 'attack' only the behaviors characteristic of the disease, and not the person who has the disease. Forcing consequences is critical because they cause a change of perspective that leads to seeking help. The consequences make it impossible for the alcoholic to deny what he has become. If we continue to adjust our behavior to the alcoholic's, rather than confronting the results of his behavior with a talk about alcoholism, we get nowhere."

"Hopefully," said Jason, "the consequences get his attention before he goes off a cliff. If anyone provides a soft landing for the alcoholic, he will continue to drink. And why shouldn't he?"

"I frequently encounter a 'conspiracy of silence' surrounding the alcoholic," said Aaron, "an office culture that studiedly ignores the pink elephant. I had a small business client who knew his company had a problem with alcoholism. When a few new employees started, the owner took me aside and asked that I say nothing about the drinking at the company. This was his company policy: 'Don't say anything, don't do anything.'

"But until alcoholism is talked about in the open, the problem won't be dealt with," Aaron sighed. "Unfortunately, that's the reality of the stigma of the disease."

"I was reading about recovery last night," said Jason. "The Hazelden Foundation asked alcoholics in recovery what turning point had set them on a path to recovery. Seventy-seven percent said a friend or relative had intervened."[17]

"They were lucky," Aaron replied, "that someone cared enough to raise their bottom. Studies confirm that earlier interruption of the disease produces an effective recovery with fewer relapses."

"The statistics I read indicated that relatively few people actually seek recovery on their own," said Jason.

"The overall numbers are dismal," Aaron agreed. "That's why I focus on what's immediately around me and my clients. I've seen statistics that say 10, maybe 15 percent, of drinkers have alcoholism, and only 10 percent of those ever seek help for their drinking issues. Even then, only 10 percent of those ever stay sober 18 months."[18]

"I read that, too," said Jason. "I suppose that a lot of alcoholics just eke out their existences while the disease progresses."

"That's right," replied Aaron. "Hitting bottom, where one is ready to act, to seek an alternative, is relatively rare among alcoholics in general. Some 85 percent are 'functioning' alcoholics. Sadly, functioning means living a life of struggle and lost potential. Many suffer from ongoing depression. Every day, about 350 alcoholics find a bottom in death."

"It seems to follow," said Jason, "if alcoholics get help when they hit bottom, it is in the interest of everyone around the alcoholic to raise the bottom, to stop sugar-coating the truth of the disease and its attendant negative behaviors."

"Definitely," Aaron nodded earnestly. "At the same time, it's important for friends, families, and employers to stay true to principles of genuine help: *dis*enable, remove any cushions, and, at the same time, respect the person."

"Just a short time ago I thought that alcoholism was a private matter, none of an employer's business," said Jason. "I see how people believe the argument that, in a free country, people have the 'right' to be an alcoholic. But the problem is that the drinker who crosses the line from casual drinking to alcoholism starts hurting others—taking them down with him."

"Privacy is always a delicate matter, but the harm alcoholics do to themselves and to others is too important to ignore," said Aaron. "It's a public health issue, like secondhand smoke and STDs. The alcoholic, even the suspected alcoholic, must be held responsible and accountable for his actions. The alcoholic has a responsibility to recover if his drinking harms others. And that may even be a moral responsibility. But the problem is that, in the early stage, alcoholics can rarely see their real problem, and, in the middle stage, they deny their declining circumstances. Such facts suggest that family, friends, coworkers, and employers all need to participate in proposing to the alcoholic the only known solution to alcoholism—total abstinence from any consumption."

*

*A woman goes to a friend's funeral.
After the service, she asks the man's
aunt, "What a shame; how did he die?"
"Cirrhosis," she laments.
"That's terrible!
Did he ever try to quit drinking?"
"Oh, no," the aunt replied.
"It never got that bad."*

*

"How do you talk to an alcoholic in denial?" asked Jason.

"Very carefully," Aaron cautioned. "You want to be honest without breaking rapport, without sacrificing the relationship entirely. There's an old saying that's fairly accurate: 'You can always tell an alcoholic, but you can't tell him much.'

"After you have fully ceased enabling the alcoholic, when he is in the middle of a crisis of negative consequences, is an ideal time to approach him," Aaron said. "Dulling the blade may help: Instead of saying 'Frank, you're an alcoholic,' it might be better to say, 'You're exhibiting the behaviors, and suffering the problems, of someone with the disease of alcoholism,' or words to that effect. That can start the education process. Better yet, if you know a recovering alcoholic, bring the two together. An alcoholic in recovery has a special credibility and can create a unique bond with a problem drinker. He can talk about the disease in a non-threatening way, usually by discussing his own struggles and recovery."

"Raising the issue is the right thing to do," said Jason, a bit uncomfortably, "but it feels very difficult."

"Unfortunately," Aaron nodded, "the right thing to do sometimes feels like the wrong thing to do. It's normal to be uncomfortable and lack confidence, even when we know what needs to be done. We have to distance ourselves from our emotions and do what *is* right rather than what *feels* right. Fortunately, the accumulation of negative consequences can help set the stage, so the alcoholic may be looking for answers and open to what we have to say.

"The old school of alcoholism intervention taught that you can't help an alcoholic until he wants help," said Aaron. "Today we know that, if we can succeed in raising the alcoholic's bottom, he will seek help earlier. If he continues to perceive more suffering in drinking than in sobriety, he will come to value sobriety for its own sake.

"There are many ways to intervene in alcoholism," said Aaron. "All have one principle in common: Zero tolerance for drinking alcohol or using other drugs, and zero tolerance for irresponsible and negative behaviors.

"Employers are in a unique position to truly help the alcoholic, after, of course, first taking steps to protect their business interests," said Aaron. "Employers can raise the bottom, but first they must stop enabling. Employers must make sure the alcoholic fully experiences the consequences of all his dysfunctional behaviors so that the sober alternative begins to look better and better."

Aaron went on to share some guidelines for dealing with suspected alcoholics at work:

1. Don't do for the alcoholic what he should do for himself. Violating this principle allows and encourages the alcoholic to think that alcohol isn't causing his problems.
2. Don't put favorable spins on situations. Don't lie, deflect attention, cover up, or make excuses for the alcoholic's behavior or its results.
3. Make and keep the possible alcoholic accountable. Don't 'lower the bar' for him by shifting responsibilities or assigning tasks to others. (This is, in fact, an instance of learned helplessness.) Making the alcoholic's job easier lessens the effect of his behavior's consequences and leads him to believe that his behavior isn't the issue.
4. Don't give or loan money, or provide payroll advances. This restriction includes any emergency funds for such things as a mortgage, the rent, and car payments. The alcoholic who loses his car may cry, "I can't get to work without a car," but public transit is a reality for many employees in America.
5. Never provide bail money, hire lawyers, or pay fines for an alcoholic's illegal acts. He must experience the full consequences of his behavior.
6. Avoid after-hours socializing or drinking with alcoholic employees.
7. Make good your word and enforce consequences. Establish clear boundaries and requirements, and when violated, implement clear and uncompromising consequences.
8. Don't argue about alcohol. Such debate only creates a wedge in your relationship.
9. Report possibly impaired or addicted professionals to their respective licensing organizations, particularly if they have an alcohol-related arrest.
10. Forbid the alcoholic's drinking at any company function.

"That's quite a list," said Jason. "It makes me think of the old saying: The bend in the road is not the end of the road, unless you don't take the turn."

The two consultants left for their day at Coyle's, which lasted a bit longer than usual. When they adjourned to their favorite Starbucks around 4:45 p.m., they found, to Aaron's surprise and Jason's delight, Jason's wife Lisa, who had just finished a meeting of her own with a prospective client.

After Jason introduced Lisa to his mentor, she said, "You're having another session on alcoholism, aren't you?"

"Yes," Aaron replied. "In fact, we should be finishing up today."

"Jason comes home buzzing every evening with the new things he's learned from you," said Lisa.

Aaron smiled at his protégé and said, "I like that—it's gratifying when people really catch on to the things I try to teach." Turning back to Lisa, he asked if she would join them, an invitation she accepted happily.

The trio placed their orders at the bar—Lisa, still zipping on caffeine from her late afternoon meeting, chose a cup of green tea—and then they took a table near the front window, where they could watch the autumn sun setting over the busy city.

Sipping her tea, Lisa said, "I've been intrigued since that first night you called, when we were still unpacking, and you asked Jason to start researching alcoholism in the workplace—how did you become aware of this problem?"

Aaron smiled modestly. "That's something of a story in and of itself," he said.

A sudden thought seem to take Lisa. She sat up a bit, drew closer to Aaron over the table and said, "You're not an alcoholic, are you?"

"Lisa!" Jason cried, his eyes wide as he looked at her with something close to horror.

But Aaron only laughed, surprised and amused by Jason's stunned reaction. Smiling at the younger man, he said, "I see some of us still labor under the stigma and misinformation that surround the disease."

Jason flushed with embarrassment, then said, "Well, I mean—"

But Aaron brushed away the faux pas with a wave of his hand. Then he turned to Lisa and said, "Actually, I prefer to say that I have alcoholism. That way, I'm not defined by the disease but by the recovery."

"I never thought of it that way," said Jason.

"Neither did I," Aaron smiled, "until I had to."

Lisa gazed at him and shook her head slightly. "This is fascinating," she said. "You wouldn't want to tell me what happened, would you?"

"Certainly," Aaron said. "It keeps the memory green."

Jason said, "This will be the story of your 'bottom' with drinking, won't it?"

"Exactly," said Aaron.

"Were you on a job?" said Lisa. "Or had you lost your work?"

"No, I was on a job," said Aaron, "but it was the only client I had or had even heard from in four months. They were a national company that sold and installed window film. I'd been brought in to straighten out ongoing cash-flow problems. Of course, that meant looking at the books.

"I was drinking quite heavily, of course, and up to all the usual tricks—breath mints, mouthwash, Teabury gum—but I had been

*

*A bottom is when
you stop digging.*

*

feeling worse and worse for quite a while. I had started leaving a jigger of vodka beside my bed before I passed out at night, so I'd have a drink ready to kick start me in the morning."

"Vodka, because it has no odor," said Lisa.

"It does when you sweat it," said Aaron.

Jason shook his head in amazement as Aaron continued: "I'd already gone through the moment of asking myself, 'Am I an alcoholic?' It was a question I couldn't bring myself to answer. I knew the answer, of course, but I couldn't yet say it, not even to myself. Because I didn't know what I would do if I had to stop drinking. I'd heard of treatment centers and groups like Alcoholics Anonymous, but I could not imagine that anything in the world would work for me the way that alcohol did."

"Even when it wasn't working so well anymore," said Lisa.

"You've got the picture," said Aaron.

Jason leaned forward with interest. "What finally broke through the denial?"

"A couple of graphs," said Aaron. "I was in the company library, going over their accounting, and I came across a report that featured overlays. You know, graphs printed on transparencies. The report was laid out to be read from right to left. I turned the first page and saw a thick red line plunging down and to the right, and it made me think of my income. Of course, I had long since started hitting my retirement fund to pay bills—and buy liquor. I sat there in the library for a moment just looking at that graph. I felt hot, suddenly, and I could feel my heart beating. I turned the next page.

"I didn't even bother to read the caption on the graph. It showed a blue line that rose rapidly from the left corner to the upper right. And

I thought of my drinking—the skyrocket course it had followed over the years since I had my first beer.

"It was the Big X, you see? X marks the spot, they say, and I knew I was on it. I sat there sweating and I whispered to myself, 'I'm a drunk. I'm an alcoholic.'" Aaron sat back in his chair. Lisa and Jason leaned closer. Aaron said, "I didn't know it then, but I'd had my last drink that morning."

"And that was your bottom," said Lisa.

"That was the beginning of my bottom," said Aaron, sitting up a little. "I went back to my hotel that night and poured out what alcohol I had. Of course, I couldn't sleep without drinking, so I didn't sleep. And the first thought that came to me was that I hadn't really gone to sleep in years—I'd always drunk until I passed out—and I called that 'going to sleep.'

"Memories flooded my mind all night long. The more I thought about it, the more I realized that I had been drinking alcoholically from very near the beginning."

"You started seeing through your rational lies," said Jason.

"Sobriety does that," Aaron smiled slightly. "Even the kind of tenuous sobriety I had that night. Until then, I never realized how much I had changed. As I rested on the hotel bed and saw myself, over the years, becoming more and more withdrawn and isolated, restless, irritable, and depressed. Behind all these problems was the cause: the simple desire to be alone and drink in peace the way I wanted to—the alcoholic way.

"The elaborate excuses I'd made up to explain my financial decline and my lack of motivation all seemed to crumble under this painful, new honesty. I'd always been pleased that other people weren't aware of the extent of my drinking, but now I saw with crystal clarity that I had actually been hiding the drinking for years.

"The way an alcoholic does."

Lisa said, "So it was an emotional experience."

"Right," said Aaron. "Nothing melodramatic—no flashing police lights, no wrecked cars. Just a wrecked human being." He sipped his coffee. "I said three words that were totally unnatural to me: I need help."

"How long did it take you to recover?" said Lisa.

"Good question," Aaron smiled. "In some ways, I'm still recovering; and I'll go on recovering as long as I live. But that first year, of course, was a big milestone. I hadn't spent a year without a drink since I started.

"And I saw even more of the truth as time went by. I saw how the egotism of my early-stage alcoholism propelled me to best-selling authorship, popularity on the lecture circuit, and a career as a highly paid consultant. And I saw the results of all the other character traits of the disease as well.

"I went to Alcoholics Anonymous, and I studied alcoholism. Over time, I began to see my work as a consultant in a different light. I could see myself in others now, and I saw behavior that seemed consistent with alcoholism.

"I began to look back at situations and clients from the past, and I saw that alcoholism—other people's—had been a part of the picture all along. When I learned about the progressive nature of the disease, I saw how certain of my clients had succeeded fabulously, only to

*

*I got sober when I
was beaten teachable.*

*

suffer a rapid decline. Alcoholism had never even been discussed in those cases, though it clearly was a factor." Aaron shook his head a little sadly.

Lisa said, "You *are* fortunate, from what Jason has told me."

Aaron nodded. "I have a close friend who used to be a prominent eye surgeon. He built one of the largest and best run eye-surgery facilities in America. He always lived large, and incurred a lot of debt. That kind of success is typical of many early-stage alcoholics. So was his decline. It really is a progressive disease. His career ended with a DUI that left him facing disciplinary action from the state medical board. They ordered him to abstain from all alcohol and submit to weekly urine tests. He fought it, and in the end, they gave him a choice between his career and his drinking."

"Please don't say it," said Lisa.

"He chose alcohol," Aaron replied. "His money will enable him to drink himself to death in relative comfort."

"But you made it," said Jason.

Aaron looked across the table at him. "I haven't had a drink today," he said. "That's 'making it.'"

"Do you still want it?" said Lisa.

"No," Aaron shook his head. "The desire left me rather quickly—some people struggle with it for years. As I say, I'm a fortunate man." He sat back. "It hasn't been a sleigh ride, of course. I remember the second year I was sober, I suffered from all kinds of alcoholic emotions and thoughts."

*

*Sobriety is not for people who need it—
it's for people who want it.*

*Addiction is about me.
Recovery is about we.*

*There is more to being sober
than quitting drinking*
*

"I have a college friend who's a recovering alcoholic," said Lisa, "and she's told me a little about what she calls 'dry drunks.' Is that the sort of thing you're talking about?"

Aaron leaned forward. "First, you need to understand that a recovering alcoholic is abstinent, not cured. Think of the disease as in remission, always ready for the alcoholic to reactivate it by drinking. What recovering people mean by the word *sober* is being healthy emotionally and spiritually—being of 'sound mind'—above and beyond abstinence itself.

"Healing doesn't occur simply by maintaining abstinence, and it certainly doesn't happen overnight—or over a matter of weeks or months," Aaron explained. "It takes a long time and a lot of work to heal the spirit and the mind. There's a whole program of recovery to be implemented once abstinence is achieved, but the alcoholic absolutely must stop drinking altogether in order to achieve full-fledged sobriety."

"So there is a substantial difference between the dry drunk and the actually recovering alcoholic," Aaron explained. "The dry drunk abstains from drinking, but typically doesn't change his thinking or behavior significantly beyond that. In fact, his behaviors may deteriorate even more. But one change that results over time in recovery is an observable sense of humility. Remember the difference in the two high achievers? A person in recovery gradually evolves into someone different from the guy we knew in the drinking days; his values, priorities, and general demeanor shift. Recovery reaches into a deeper level, emotionally and spiritually, than abstinence can. Many recovery programs, like the one offered by Alcoholics Anonymous, the original 12-Step Program, reach to deeper levels of spirituality, feeling, and personal responsibility."

Aaron continued. "The recovering alcoholic, whether at work or at home, goes through a right-sizing of himself. He is reversing the extremes we talked about before, of ego-inflating behaviors, distorted perceptions, and impaired judgment. He experiences a reduction of his ego while he undergoes a restoration of his self-esteem. Humility and honesty take the place of a big ego and a self-centered view of the world.

"When we think of others, like our coworkers and friends, we need to ask ourselves this question: If the situation were reversed, what ultimately would we want them to do for us?" said Aaron. "If my friends and coworkers could see that I was headed for an alcoholic train wreck, would I want them to remain passive and tell themselves 'there isn't anything I can do'? Or would I want them to bring on, as they say, the tough love?"

"I'd be angry with them," Jason said, "but if I did recover, I'd have to thank my friends. And if I remained on the downward spiral, at least they could have clear consciences—they did try to make a difference."

"When we deal honestly with alcoholism by enforcing the consequences and providing information and alternatives, the alcoholic isn't the only one who benefits," said Aaron. "The family, friends, coworkers, and employers all gain. So, for that matter, do other drivers out on the roads. And we can add to that benefit the decrease in the direct and indirect costs to business, medicine, and society in general. Alcoholism is rampant. Awareness and education will help remove the stigma of the disease, just as education campaigns did for depression.

"In the meantime, we have to ask ourselves tough questions," Aaron said. "If we recognize alcoholism, or even suspect the likelihood of it, why do we not act when the alcoholic continues to deteriorate, harming himself and taking others down with him? The sooner we intervene with alternatives, the better the likelihood of arresting the disease early on and producing a lasting recovery. Why wait until too late, when permanent damage is done or a head-on collision, for instance, has claimed several lives? The disease is *always* progressive. It may appear to pause in its advance, but it moves inevitably forward, toward health problems, depression, accidents, and suicides.

"Here, then," said Aaron, "is the challenge businesses, coworkers, friends and family must face: How far do we let the disease progress before we take action? Do we wait for a doctor's instruction to intervene, or a cop's, or a judge's? Do we delay until a fatal collision or a suicide attempt? Do we just watch a human being deteriorate to the point that effective recovery is *more* difficult? Why do we wait for him to kill himself or someone else?

"The challenge for employers, coworkers, friends, and family is simple: Do we care enough to raise the bottom?"

*

There comes a time
when Silence is Betrayal.

*

Endnotes

[1] SAMHSA's Office of Applied Studies (OAS) provides the latest national data on (1) alcohol, to-bacco, marijuana and other drug abuse, (2) drug-related emergency department episodes and medical examiner cases, and (3) the nation's substance abuse treatment system. For latest data on alcoholism, visit www.oas.samhsa.gov.

[2] Drugs in the Workplace: Research and Evaluation Data Volume II, National Institute on Drug Abuse. Research Monograph 100, 1990.

[3] Substance Abuse and Mental Health Services Administration (SAMHSA) Office of Applied Studies (OAS) For latest data on alcoholism, visit www.oas.samhsa.gov.

[4] Drugs in the Workplace: Research and Evaluation Data Volume II, National Institute on Drug Abuse. Research Monograph 100, 1990.

[5] Ketcham, Katherine and William F. Ashbury, with Mel Schulstad and Arthur P. Ciaramicoli, Ed.D., Ph.D., *Beyond the Influence: Understanding and Defeating Alcoholism,* New York, NY: Bantam Books, 2000.

[6] Thorburn, Doug, *Drunks, Drugs & Debits*, Northridge, CA: Galt Publishing 2000.

[7] Ketcham, Katherine and William F. Ashbury, with Mel Schulstad and Arthur P. Ciaramicoli, Ed.D., Ph.D., *Beyond the Influence: Understanding and Defeating Alcoholism,* New York, NY: Bantam Books, 2000.
For more information on how the body metabolizes alcohol, see pp 19-26.

[8] Thorburn, Doug, *How to Spot Hidden Alcoholics,* Northridge, CA: Galt Publishing 2004

[9] Smoking Status as a Clinical Indicator for Alcohol Misuse in U.S. Adults; Sherry A. McKee, PhD; Tracy Falba, PhD; Stephanie S. O'Malley, PhD; Jody Sindelar, PhD; Patrick G. O'Connor, MD, MPH *Archives of Internal Medicine* 2007;167:716-721.

[10] See above.

[11] Thorburn, Doug, *Drunks, Drugs & Debits*, Northridge, CA: Galt Publishing 2000 pages 88-89.

[12] Thorburn, Doug, *How to Spot Hidden Alcoholics,* Northridge, CA: Galt Publishing 2004

[13] Numerous studies and Surveillance Reports from the National Institute on Alcohol Abuse and Alcoholism of the National Institutes of Health.

[14] Collins, Jim. *Good to Great: Why Some Companies Make the Leap… and Others Don't,* New York:HarperBusiness 2001

[15] Califano, Jr, Joseph A., *High Society*, New York, NY: PublicAffairs, a member of the Perseus Books Group. 2007

[16] Twerski, MD, Abraham J. *Addictive Thinking: Understand Self-Deception,* Center City, MN: Hazelden. Pp 102-104.

[17] Bruce Cotter, *When They Won't Quit,* Hunt Valley, MD: Holly Hill Publishing 2002

[18] Califano, Jr, Joseph A., *High Society*, New York, NY: PublicAffairs, a member of the Perseus Books Group. 2007.

For more information on alcoholism and recovery,
visit www.raisethebottom.com

Acknowledgments

This book stands on the shoulders of the work of many great researchers and authors on alcoholism. In particular, the work of Doug Thorburn introduced me to the behavioral distinctions of the stages of alcoholism. Much of Part 2 is an adaptation of behavioral clues from his book *Drunks, Drugs & Debits*. Authors Katherine Ketcham and Abraham J. Twerski, MD, greatly influenced my knowledge on alcoholism and the alcoholic mind. Ken Blanchard's writing style in his numerous books inspired the story style of this book.

Ed Boggan contributed a great deal with his skillful editing as well as his insights and perspective on alcoholism. The brilliant Robert Prechter, Jr. provided precise final edits and suggestions. Jody Dyer, the smartest entrepreneur I know, shared countless business insights through our many lunches. His wife Ella provided generous proofreading, feedback, and encouragement.

I especially thank the many alcoholics in and out of recovery who have shared themselves so fully and honestly with me. They continue to teach me.

There are many teachers, mentors, advisors, or friends that I want to acknowledge, including: Ralph Berkeley, MD, the late Jerry Cates, the late John Coggins, Tom Crum, the late John Denver, David Dulaney, MD, Bruce Kramer, Terry Nowicki, Clay Porter, and Ed Sullivan.

And lastly, a great thank you to my brother and sister, Allen Jackson and Mary Ellen Jackson for their love and support. They still wonder what I really do for a living.

About the Author

Arthur Jackson has over twenty years experience as a business and marketing consultant. He has a diverse background and a broad range of experience, including politics, entertainment, non-profits, health care, business start-ups, e-commerce, and information technology. Arthur is a graduate of the University of Georgia and lives in Marietta, Georgia.